MEMORIAL

FRANCIS STUART

RAVEN ARTS PRESS / DUBLIN
COLIN SMYTHE / BUCKS.

This book is published by

THE RAVEN ARTS PRESS
P.O. Box 1430
Finglas
Dublin 11
Republic of Ireland

COLIN SMYTHE LTD.
P.O. Box 6
Gerrards Cross
Buckinghamshire
England

First published in 1973 by Martin, Brian & O'Keeffe Ltd., London.

ISBN Raven Arts Press 0 906897 87 4 (softback)
0 906897 88 2 (hardback)

Colin Smythe 0 86140 224 3
0 86140 223 5

The Raven Arts Press receives financial assistance from the Arts Council/*An Chomhairle Ealaíon,* Dublin. The author and publishers would like to thank Mr Timothy O'Keeffe for his co-operation in the re-issue of this book.

Cover design by John Farman. Portrait of Francis Stuart by Thomas Ryan, R.H.A. Jacket design by Syd Bluett. Printing and binding by Confidential Report Printing, Dublin. Hardback binding by Duffy Book Binders, Dublin.

PART ONE

To M,
with love

ONE

Herra, this is the report I once promised you.

How start? With something neutral, which isn't easy to hit on where every object seems highly charged. What about the old Rolls? It had taken me half across Europe to your mother's house in the elegant, suburban street. Recognising car and driver as from another world (a matter of suspicion seeing she had already come up against another such refugee in you?) she guessed it was the expected visitor and came to greet him with outstretched hand. Which I hesitated to take in my journey-grimed one.

Mrs. Friedlander had invited me to her house when she heard I was coming to the city to give a talk to a literary society to which she belonged. I had been asked in the slack season at a time of no local cultural stir because, I suppose, my last novel had achieved some notoriety. 'Should be treated with the silent contempt it deserves,' wrote one critic in quite a long review.

'Could we talk about your book later? I'm waiting for the story to start.'

Some of your interruptions are factual, some imagined by me.

Inside the house: handshakes, felicitations, everything welcoming, relaxed, except for the eyes fixed on me from a corner of the room, yours, I mean, not Lazarella's that were regarding me from under a small table.

Yes, I'm coming to the point: your appearance at the door of my room as I was tidying myself for the late evening meal with the ginger cat in your arms.

'Lazarella has come to say *bonne nuit.*'

The effect of the French words added to the almost perfect English wasn't as intended which, I suppose, was just to draw my attention in the midst of all the distractions; I thought: What a little show-off!

'Only Lazarella?'

'Both of us.'

'Do you go to bed so early?'

'I get up soon after five to deliver newspapers.'

'Oh.'

'I give the money to a home for stray animals.'

'Can I come too?'

'I'll knock on your door when it's time to get up.'

Shall I tell you what I dreamt that night? I was wafted on one of those conducted flights to erotic zones, this time, in terrestrial terms, to the far north.

A tap on the wall of an igloo. The non-answer deepening the snowy silence to expectation force eight, and rising slowly. Tiptoeing (in snowshoes) into the chill gloom to catch a murmur from under a pile of reindeer skins: For mercy's sake, come and warm me!

Console, comfort, but no precipitate fondling. What had we here? An Esquimo belle in her early teens whose parents, on a business trip to Anchorage, had got held up by . . .

Thoroughly thaw out one side of the frozen form, turn it round, not trying to distinguish too closely front from back. . . .

You left your bike at home and, the less alert part of me still in the chill twilight of the other cell or cubicle, we sailed off on the first of our memorable expeditions in the Rolls. Having collected the papers and reached the first of your allotted streets, you started down it at a near-run, what looked like a postman's discarded satchel over one shoulder and a Lufthansa bag with the cat in it slung from the other.

The entrance halls of apartment houses with their metal rows of letter boxes and odour of past grandeur turned stale and slightly dank. An occasional dash through a courtyard and up flights of stairs to push through old-fashioned, brass-bound slits in mahogany doors, copies of their papers to apparently privileged subscribers.

Into one of the apertures you thrust your hand and part of your narrow wrist after ringing the bell. What was taking place on the other side of the heavy door? Had a greedy mouth descended on to your upwards-turned palm? Was my dream being fulfilled with another dreamer?

When you withdrew your hand it was grasping a small paper packet. You unwrapped what looked like some thin, roughly-rolled cheroots.

'Never seen a joint before?'

We sat on the landing with our feet on the descending stair and breakfasted off sandwiches you fished from the bottom of the depleted satchel and Lazarella emerged from her travelling bag and licked the fish from between one of them.

'It seems to me . . .'

'Don't pretend to be shocked.'

Even at that early stage there was a very private line between us.

'You don't smoke the stuff?'

Munching, you said something I didn't catch and probably wasn't meant to. Indistinct murmurs, as I soon saw, had a part in your system of communication, not just with animals but also with me.

'Too bloody young.'

'I started having my periods last year.'

The distant clatter of an early bus and, on my part, silence. Which was broken by you, and properly so, with: 'I read your book.'

Ah, my precious, maligned book that had given you the courage to appear at the door of my room the previous evening!

Perhaps at a sign from you that I missed, the cat jumped lightly back into its basket and the crumbs scattered from your short skirt as you jumped up just as lithely; about to stoop and step in front of me into the bridal car, was one of the less fantastic thoughts that I immediately cancelled as I rose stiffly. Back in the leafy street with the occasional empty spaces between the tall houses, lingering weed-grown memories of a long-ago disaster, some screened by advertisement hoardings.

Attention Esquimo Belles! Best value in fur-lined nighties.

In the morning, handshakes again, but from you a dark and stormy glance illumined by a smile. Note: I hadn't been able to find the silver and, I think, onyx cuff links I wore with my one elegant shirt, now elegantly dirty.

TWO

Good morning and greetings to you at the school on the shore of the Swiss lake to which you'd been transferred from the one nearer home after the disappearance of Lazarella—that I only heard of much later—and, on a less tragic level, some delinquencies connected, I imagined, with the stuff you'd withdrawn through the letter-box. I'd send you a prickly holly leaf from the tree that grows on one of the two graves in my garden if I knew your address, though the two granite slabs that I'd hauled down a mountain and into the boot of the car, one of the most precious of its many cargoes, and set up under a grassy bank, were not really grave stones. The larger one commemorated those few friends who for what seems a brief period shared with me not only the gift of breathing but a related manner of feeling and perceiving. The other stone preserved, for none of course but me, the memory of some vanished creatures, all small, furry and whiskered.

I don't want to give you a picture of the grey-headed writer communing with the past in the peace of his country seclusion. As well as my dreams and my waking obsessions, always excessive, often painful, there were shames and weaknesses. There were times when I scanned the literary supplements to see some reference to myself, to try to reassure myself that, as a writer, I hadn't vanished utterly from the public ken.

If I was ever mentioned it was as 'Professor Sugrue', having once taught in a foreign university, or as the distinguished lecturer, having two or three times in my life given a talk in a public hall, or as the dramatist, on the strength of a single play.

Shall I tell you of those hours of resentment on mornings when my steps took me along interior mudflats at lower-than-low tide in a search for my initials (F.F.S.) scrawled in the wet sand? Or of the long winter evenings when I lifted the telephone receiver and, without dialling, listened to the purring and, for the sake of breaking the daylong silence, murmured something into it, anything, 'the humming birds are humming in the trees'. Or, once, spoke your name and waited, hearing the echo of distant waves in the black, land-locked shell.

Very occasionally the instrument did give the shrill signal indicating that someone was in contact with its hidden—like the invisible bait at the end of a fishing line—extremity. But never the fish that I'd glimpsed in the shadows, fragile, elusive, swift and wild. Until, that is, on the least of all likely mornings—I had my ways of defining the varying degrees of the impossible—the phone in the corner of the kitchen under the Seurat reproduction rang and the voice was yours. Saying it didn't matter what into the parched shell, touching it with the revivifying tide. Saying, as the sense came through the shock of the sound, that you were here in the city with a group of girls from your Swiss establishment on a tour of this off-shore island. You were ready to play truant from a sight-seeing drive round the town that afternoon if . . . If what?

If I'd been just a little slower than I was in registering the distress signal you'd have rung off; or wouldn't you? The wave withdrew from the quickly drying shell and I thought: it's on the turn. What is, for the love of Christ? The tide of life—if you deal in images, they are there in crises too—of my life.

At the last minute I asked what you had in mind.

'I'd like, if *you* like, to visit you.'

Was the hall of the hotel empty or full? If I'd noticed on entering, the memory was obliterated, and all else that happened immediately before catching sight of you. Even the you I'd come to meet vanished and this was the girl of a year later, time in which to change at her age.

The moment you sat beside me in the Rolls you were the phantom that creeps before dawn into the old monk's cell, in this case a mobile one, to reveal what, for all his meditation, he has never been granted a vision of: the beatitude of youth.

When I opened the door and followed you into the cottage I looked at the clock in the kitchen as a way of keeping some of my bearings. Then as I turned to the window above the sink with an idea of showing you the view that in all weathers and at the various hours of the day was my most familiar one, I sensed it was altered and ruined.

Small dark remnants were scattered over the lawn between ditch and laurels which, as I was collecting and putting them together again in futile imagination, I recognised as the remains of a brood of leverets that the cats had discovered in the bramble hedge and ravaged.

We were just in time to rescue from under the bushes one small object intact, speckled-grey with black, sideways-set eyes, dull with terror or resignation. How evoke the sensation shared between us, wordless and as unforgettable as first-time sex, while preventing the massacre from being total?

You let me hold the fragile yet, as far as I could judge, undamaged creature while you made a nest in the carton in which the Japanese binoculars I'd lately bought had come. And you found, among the phials with stained, indecipherable labels in the small medicine cupboard on the bathroom wall, a glass device I'd once used to drop lotion into tired eyes.

You held the leveret to your breast while the till-then hidden mouth fastened on the nozzle. It was then I saw the short thread-like scar on the underside of the wrist of the hand that was feeding it. With the fur rippling round the baby hare's muzzle and to the faint sibilance of its sucking, our eyes met. A sign between us that couldn't be put in words, communicating what language isn't fashioned for. On my part a recognition that you had been places that, in a long life, I'd only skirted imaginatively.

You said you'd phone to the mistress in charge of the group with an excuse for not returning to the hotel that night. What excuse? No matter; the sooner you phoned the better. That you'd come with others in charge of a school mistress, and that your absence wouldn't be taken quietly, were considerations whose relevance was eroded by what was happening. And next morning, though we didn't see them, there was news in the papers of a foreign schoolgirl's disappearance from her school group on a tour of the country.

That wasn't the end of my folly. I took you to dine that night with neighbours, friends, as I had been credulously thinking of them, and you wore the bracelets that you'd taken off before lifting up the leveret to feed and hadn't put on again.

At first there wasn't any suspicion in the air, just our hostess's perfume and a whiff of Continental cooking afloat in the room and roosting on our shoulders, while we sipped aperitifs, you one too, and I didn't warn you how strong they were, the bracelets not hiding the scars in one wrist when you raised the glass.

'You never met my grand-daughter, my son's second daughter, good God, yes, or rather no, she's on a first visit.' But when the question was put to you, joking, semi-casual, deadly earnest, you told them (and it was marvellous): *Ich bin die Zucker Puppe aus dem Bauchtanz Gruppe!* Just what was needed to show them up and, of course, to ensure your being traced. I'm just the sugar dolly from a belly-dance group.

Returning after midnight you entered the cottage first and stood stock still just inside the living room. From over your shoulder I saw the small out-of-place object on the paler carpet. Had the cats torn a scrap from the darker rug or been playing with a piece of coal from the scuttle? None of these happy and trivial normalities were going to let the nocturnal relief of homecoming set in. The small, neat remainder and reminder had been laid out and was waiting for us in the centre of the room.

What we did: the pulling out of the box that had seemed such a snug, safe place under the lower shelf of the book-case and the peering through the now obviously too-large mesh wire with which it was covered, were the futile, panic-stricken efforts of the condemned, and guilty, to escape.

A quick search of the room; nothing out of place, but

also no sign. Outside, the quietude, twice as deep for being false, of deep night.

When I had enough composure to notice details I saw the small, still-damp stain on the worn patch of carpet near the door and, dropping on my knees, two or three rain drops of blood unabsorbed, such as I'd mused over on leaves in the garden after a shower.

The trees and shrubs were awaiting the dawn that would not be delayed.

What had the weather been like the morning Mary Magdalen had gone to the tomb to sit an hour or two at the newly-sealed grave? Better there than keep shaking her head on the pillow to rid her mind of certain memories.

It had rained continuously the night of the death of the leveret and all the next morning. Shortly before the grey wet dawning they'd closed the door of the living room behind them, dragged themselves the few feet to the bedroom, undressed silently and got into the one bed.

What thoughts were you thinking as we lay side by side, fearing the new day and having, sooner or later, to start it? Ones that, as far as others were concerned, were incommunicable. For instance: that the leveret had winced at a door shut noisily.

You got up in the night and went, by way of the living room, to the bathroom. I heard the padding of your bare feet that turned to faint tapping on the linoleum. The homely sounds of a toilet flushing, a tap running, that were no longer reassuring, and, on your way back, a pause, a silence, not hard to interpret.

Mary had stood staring at the open tomb.

Three or four hours of semi-oblivion and then the leafy drive a public thoroughfare and neighbours watching from behind their hedge as I was accompanied out by civic guards and followed a few minutes later by you with a policewoman. The rest they could reconstruct in righteous horror: taken in the unspeakable repetition of the unspeakable, dragged from the desecrated bed, the sheets of which no washing machine or launderette would accept with the decently dirty linen, but spew out even if hidden at the centre of the bundle. Blessed art thou among women and . . . Was old Mrs. MacWhatadoo saying her beads?

They'll need the bloody sheets to produce at the trial.

Jesus and Mary preserve us! And scarcely a sight or sound of him during all the years he's been living here in our midst, except for his calling one of his bloody cats, and then in a kind of whisper, and strolling round his bit of garden morning and evening with the couple of queer stones set up in it.

I was taken away in the police car and it was explained to you that another was coming from the city to reunite you with your schoolfellows, although where you were actually taken to was the hospital.

The market town was *en fête* for the *Fleadh* and I heard the music as I sat on a bench in the Gardai barracks where I'd been on other occasions—once to report the illtreatment by persistent kicking of a sick calf in an effort by its owner, one of the lately head-wagging onlookers, to get it to move to a more convenient spot to die in, and be buried, than the secluded corner of the field it had chosen.

Sergeant: Names in full.
F.F.S. Fintan Francis Sugrue.
Sergeant: Occupation.
F.F.S. Recorder of improbable but true fantasies with which I hope to forge better instruments of understanding and imagining.

Which, inadequate and immoderate as it was, boiled down in the spoken word to the still-more inadequate and quite colourless: Writer.

It was my age, of course, that scandalised them most.

Or was it *your* age?

In my own eyes, in your eyes and in their eyes, I was, in each of these, a quite different person.

But the scandal wasn't all on the one side. They'd have been astonished had they had an inkling of how this monster saw them.

Their image of sex was on the back of their holy images, formed from the wrong side of the highly-coloured print. The unclean beast could thus be wallowed in as long as it was part of the hallowed picture blessed by the priest. Sanctified dirt, that's how they saw sex in marriage. Otherwise it was a wild hog with filthy, burrowing, ravaging snout to be kept out of sight, sound and, as far as practicable, scent, in a den beneath farm house or the newer double-fronted bungalows.

Where, licensed for release at the approved nocturnal hours, its mindless maulings soon became evident not just in the speed of the pregnancies but in the vulgarisation of the young wives.

Girls that had swung down the road with a free stride and an open smile for whoever passed, a year or two later trudged, with coarsened face and desensitised body, from clothes line to back door.

Not that I didn't submit myself for judgment, but not to them and their lawfully-appointed spokesmen.

It was the blanched, wet primroses that I'd noticed on the side of the road from the police car and had never seen so clearly before that spoke to me in an idiom that I accepted.

What did they say? Is that you asking somewhat sceptically; you never liked anything that might be interpreted as evasion. Be patient, I'm not dragging them in for effect. They spoke to me of a simplicity that is part of lost innocence, of my childhood, I think. But of coded and categorised morality, not a word.

What else is there to report about the proceedings at the barracks? Only what I kept from you at the time: that out of weariness or weakness, though believing it was best for us both, I signed a document that there'll be more to say about later.

THREE

Having, it seems, received the report of the doctor who examined you which corroborated your own statement that had probably startled the policewoman—though perhaps not—that 'fucking had been furthest from our minds' (slightly dishonest but entirely justified) they released me in mid-morning into the warm ashes of the new day sluggishly catching fire.

A chemical mist from spilt or exhaled alcohol hung about the place mingled with the less nauseating one of warm, damp bodies prone or in sitting postures. Seeking seclusion, I turned into a church where Mass was being celebrated.

Watching the priest at the altar my whole-hearted attention was drawn there as to a crowd round the victim of an accident. In my semi-shocked state I could associate without incongruity what in more orderly thoughts are kept strictly apart: the ancient public myth with the recent very private event.

The priest was commemorating a calamity. The obscurity in which it had taken place had been part of its pain. The Victim had been defenceless and almost friendless. Now, through centuries of over-exposure, the tragedy had been formalised and diluted. And I saw that it could only haunt me again, as it had once, by association with the utterly obscure and unpublicisable one known to nobody but you and me.

It started with tender nativity. It was the leveret sucking from the dropper and covering its muzzle with its paws when—as you explained it—it had had enough. As the priest held wide his arms with the palms inwards and slightly apart it was a frail new creature that he was displaying to my rapt gaze.

A small, nose-twitching, speckled Babe needing sleep and warmth. That is why we had left the box-manger in the sitting room, covered in wire-netting and pushed under the bottom shelf of the book-case.

As the priest elevated the Chalice I saw the drops, no more than two, on the threadbare bit of carpet.

On my return to the Gardai station in the late afternoon to read over and sign the voluntary and quite meaningless statement I'd made earlier and that they had typed in duplicate, I was given the message from your mother about meeting her and you at the local hotel that evening.

She had flown over apparently as soon as she'd heard of your disappearance and had been at the hospital in time to hear, as you put it, the news of your passing your examination.

Do you remember—will, that is, you ever forget, our reunion in the Club Arms Hotel, the rain falling outside, the orders given, not excluding a repast for the cats that, having taken with you in a travelling bag to the city, you had brought back again? We looked at each other, when your mother had gone to the toilet, in a silence that encompassed our depths of relief.

'Of course I didn't let them examine me.'

'No?'

'Calm yourself, Miss Friedlander, we only want to make sure you weren't molested.' That's how the woman doctor tried to persuade me to undress.

'Molested? How do you mean?'

Lady doctor and nurse looked at each other and were more or less satisfied.

'I told her we were with friends of yours called MacAlinden.'

'Who?'

'MacAlinden; I'd heard the name and it stuck in my mind.'

'I mean: who did you tell?'

'Mama, of course. That reassured her. Then I told her that if she tried to send me back to Switzerland, she needn't think I'd go willingly, but if they managed to drag me there I'd do more thoroughly what I did before.'

'You've been arguing your case with skill and subtlety.'

'Our case, isn't it?'

'Well . . .'

'Wait till I finish. I suggested she engage Liz Considine—who was assistant to the mistress in charge of the tour and is a fellow countrywoman of yours and who'll get the sack for my defection—as my governess, and that we stay with you at your house in the country. I made it sound big because what's grand is safe in my mother's eyes—and you'd help me in my literature study and give me religious instruction, because Liz is too Catholic to entrust me to for that.'

In the month of June (I was looking ahead) with the wind from the north-east, petals of white-thorn that turn pink as they fade are blown like sparse snow flakes at sunset across the back window of my room. Inside, the furniture and books repose in their hallowed places, the sights and faint sounds are the accustomed and hallowed ones down to the drip from the last shower into the water butt.

What will happen to all this if you and your governess move in?

I'm telling you some of my first thoughts, keeping nothing back. Oh, I'd gained some tranquillity and inner repose with age but was in danger of losing the power to risk them for the sake of a new and totally unexpected prize!

At that moment, luckily, before you guessed my brief hesitation, your mother returned and apologised to me for involving me in the wretched affair, as she called it. She told me how relieved she was at not having to try to find a new school for you, the fourth, was it, in three years, and other things too to do with your latest 'escapade' and, as you must have told her, your unannounced arrival at my 'country house'.

'What have you been telling him, girl, while I was upstairs?'

'Nothing.'

She glanced from one to the other of us with what I thought was a slight bewilderment. Had a shadow from the humid, fertile place where we meet cast its shade momentarily over her bright assurance?

One thing I'd make sure of: never again would they take us by surprise. I'd construct a defensive position, perhaps in the loft over the garage, where we could be together, your guardian agreeing, or being circumvented, without risking another outrage.

When you and Mrs. Considine arrived by taxi I was mowing the lawn between the laurels and the ditch beyond which the domain of black, tilled earth and cropped hedges began, and where it soon dawned on you wild-life found little shelter.

There were the rooms to show your governess, three in all, and to explain, in case you hadn't, that you and she would be sharing the bedroom. She'd expected something more commodious, that was clear. You, I suppose, had known what to expect and your face showed nothing, but it never did, not even when I had taken what I thought would be a long farewell under the eyes of the policewoman.

'O.K.?'

'Of course.'

Mrs. Considine was paying off the car.

'What about you?'

You didn't yet know about the haven, the citadel, the ark, as I was coming to regard it. There hadn't been time, or the time hadn't been ripe to show you the loft on your brief other visit. Nobody guessed, except the builder who'd converted it for me, and he wasn't local, that the cottage contained under its long, red-tiled roof a large room once used as a granary above the equally big barn, now a garage and storage space.

The first evening started by having its low spots. Whatever Mrs. Considine's qualifications as a teacher, her conversation was limited and would soon, I saw, be predictable. Worse, she seemed to expect most of my remarks be addressed to her.

But there were compensatory gleams. I'd provided a couple of bottles of Spanish red wine at supper and was too unnerved to keep track of into whose glass it was disappearing so quickly. I supposed I must be gulping it down as I do when I'm tense. But when we met coming and going with dishes between table and sink you whispered: 'Give her some more booze.'

A little later you left the washing-up you'd volunteered to do and your governess at the table over the other bottle I'd opened, and suggested a stroll round the garden. (You'd hardly been outside the house the other time. For one thing it had rained almost continuously and anyhow, before the fatal hour, there'd been non-stop talk only interrupted to administer milk to the leveret and to prepare a scrappy late lunch with what I had in the house for ourselves. Lack of provisions had been the main reason for taking you to dinner with these so-called friends.)

I led you down the cinder track, too narrow for us to walk abreast; in cutting back the bushes I'd only had my solitary perambulations in mind. If we didn't pause somewhere for you to admire something we'd be back at the cottage door in under four minutes, you'd set such a brisk pace. I pulled the back of your blouse to bring you to a stop by the asparagus that were just thrusting creamy pink shoots through a covering of sand.

'What is it?' You looked round, startled.

'Asparagus.'

'What?'

'Your mother said you'd disappeared from school once before.'

'Oh.'

What was to become of me if the inner repose in the face of all disturbances that I thought I'd built up over the years was to disperse at the first breath from a certain ('certain': that's priceless, you murmur) direction?

'You don't have to tell me about it.' How better make sure you would?

'It was after we'd been at a film in the town.'

'Who?'

'A few of us. A film called *Outback*. I'll never forget it.'

'About animals?'

'Yes.' A 'yes' like a moan. I waited.

'There was a scene where some drunks shoot kangaroos from a car and the ones left crouching in the bush wounded, with their strange, lovely heads low, they come back for and cut off their . . .'

'Yes.'

'They were employed by the Australian government to stop them breeding too much.'

The creak of the wings of the rooks flying through the silence.

'My friend said she had an uncle in Lausanne and, without our saying so, we both felt it would be less awful to try to come to ourselves with somebody who didn't know about the film and not have to talk about it and feel sick and guilty with the others.'

Before we returned to the house I showed you the place that I'd already planned as the hide-out, though that's not the term in which I thought of it, where we'd be safe from an outrage like the one of the previous morning.

I conducted you through the barn-garage, up the ladder, through the trap-doorway and into the big, converted loft.

'Who was it meant for?'

'For myself when I wanted to escape from my marriage without actually leaving Nancy, which, strangely, she didn't want me to, and which was financially difficult. We got some unexpected money once and I got someone I knew to do it, with me helping him, for very little compared to what it'd cost now.'

'Did you live up here?'

'For a short time before she got ill.'

'What was wrong with her?'

It wasn't to tell you about Nancy that I'd brought you here, though I might another time.

'No windows, just the skylights at the rear; from the front you'd never think there was this mini-dwelling under the roof of the barn. It used to be a granary.'

'We could live out a siege, or a flood, up here.'

'That's what I thought.'

'If it wasn't for Liz.'

FOUR

Next day we went to town and with some of the money your mother had entrusted to me for my part in your education, apart from the first of the monthly sums given to the 'housekeeper', for Christ-sake, for your and Liz's keep, I bought a projector and chose some slides.

The educational series were in cartons with such titles as: 'Great Moments in History', 'Scenes from Famous Operas', 'Cities of Europe', 'Microscopic Wonders', 'Cars and their Components'. The bored salesgirl was being helpful between yawns.

'For a girl of that age group, what about . . .'

'What about what?'

Ah, Herra, to hear you referred to casually and in passing by a sleepy shop assistant who hadn't even seen you was the chance spark sucked through a subterranean crack that set ablaze the inflammable thoughts that I'd stored away in a cool, fireproof place while doing the shopping!

'What about "Costumes through the Ages"?'

Finally I came on what I was after: 'Tales from the Old Testament'.

The girl placed a couple of the slides into a lit apparatus for me to view.

'We don't sell many of these; there'll be a reduction on them as remaindered stock.'

What was she talking about? Where was I, in a busy emporium under sub-tropic stars or with you in a tent in a Promised Land whose valleys echoed with the roar of traffic?

The second slide depicted the original haven for man and beast. Coming up to an unusually prolonged and violent rainy season.

Late that afternoon Liz Considine agreed that I should give you the first of the talks about the Bible.

You arrived punctually in the loft at the hour she had entered in her schedule and, in jeans and tartan blouse, and with hair caught back from the brow that to me reflected whatever light was still unobscured in the oncoming gloom, settled yourself on the couch.

A click, loud in the silence that had gathered round us, and the one hundred-and-fifty (I think it was) bulb burst into brilliance, imprinting in startling magnification on the pale wooden partition behind which were kitchenette, toilet and bath, the glowing torsos of bearded men bent over silvery scythes and deep-breasted women with dark, secret countenances inclined towards golden corn-sheaves.

'What is it?'

You knew what it was; you'd caught some of the fever in the air, both the ancient and the immediate, but you wanted me to tell you the words for it.

I consulted the booklet that went with the slides: 'And Reuben went in the days of wheat harvest and found mandrakes in the field and brought them to his mother, Leah.'

'Which is Reuben?'

'Just a minute.'

Consult text, but no long delay or mood might be dispersed.

'Bottom left hand corner.'

'Where's his mother?'

'Leah? She enters in the next picture.'

'Please show it.'

'There. "Then Rachel said to Leah, give me, I pray thee, of thy son's mandrakes. And she said unto her . . ."'

'Let's get it straight. Who's speaking to who?'

'Herra, what grammar!'

'This isn't an English lesson.'

'The sisters are talking. The situation is this: Jacob, married to Leah by a trick of her father's, is in love with the younger girl, Rachel.'

'I'd like to be Rachel.'

I didn't ask why nor could you have said because the remark was instinctive, a desire for identification with the evident heroine.

'"And she said unto her, is it a small matter that thou hast taken my husband? And wouldst thou take away my son's mandrakes also. And Rachel said, therefore he shall lie with thee to-night for thy son's mandrakes."'

'That's immoral.'

'Immoral?'

'Mixing business with sex.'

'"And Jacob came out of the field in the evening, and Leah went out to meet him and said, thou must come in unto me . . ."'

I'd put down the booklet that had accompanied the slides and was reading from the same school bible from which these sentences had first case their spell over me.

A shadow fell over the loft as I slid the next slide into

the beam of the projector. The desert at night, sleeping flocks, the huddle of tents under the stars.

'"He went in unto her and knew her."'

These words had once obsessed and disturbed me as I'd despaired of ever gaining this mysterious knowledge. What effect would they have on you?

'What an old-fashioned way of putting it!'

The cultivation of the garden had for long been one of the ways I hoped to keep myself 'sane'. Between digging and weeding I took a rest at one of the two granite slabs. Sometimes I could almost sink into the silence where those whom the stones commemorated were gone. These were present in a very secluded corner of a remembering mind and, in most cases, nowhere else in a world that had once been theirs. There was J.L., less completely traceless than some because he'd been a writer, though an obscure one, and one of his books might still occasionally be taken from a shelf somewhere on a rainy day. I too became patient and undemanding in their company as they stood once more upright, or crept or sped silently, man or beast, in this latest of the brief resurrections that would one day cease.

The garden got dug and weeded, groundsel, dandelion, the bright green tufts of grass were uprooted while I passed from the company of the dead with the regained detachment and quietude in which the novel I was writing could grow.

When your next bible lesson was due again I invited Liz Considine to accompany you to the loft, rather to your disgust. I was thinking of the plan to forestall or delay what I foresaw as the dangers ahead for which some beguiling of your governess would be needed. Though your mother had returned home apparently satisfied with an arrangement she hadn't bothered to look into too closely, I knew I was still suspect in the eyes of the law.

With the inkling we seemed to have of each other's secrets, did an indication of the plan begin to dawn on you as the first slide of the new series was projected on the wooden wall? An object in course of construction, open and ribbed at the top. I was expecting you to ask: what on earth is it? But no, not a word; instead, a hush in which I was conscious of the sudden intensity of your thoughts.

'Man, and woman's, second (counting the earlier, somewhat discredited Adam and Eve report) attempt at self-salvage in a hostile situation.'

The fact that it was my own narrative style I was using and not that of the brochure was to substantiate your surmise. But having, as I imagined, these vital secrets with you right under the nose of Liz Considine, I read out the relevant passage for her sake: 'And God saw the wickedness of man was great in the earth, and that every imagination of the thoughts of his heart was only evil continually. And it repented the Lord that he had made man of the earth and it grieved him at his heart. . . . But Noah found grace in the eyes of the Lord.'

'I like nothing better than listening to these old tales,' said your governess, 'that many people think irrelevant or in need of up-dating.'

The next slide showed the ark as a barnlike building in a still-unthreatened, pastoral setting.

'Note the entrance placed unusually high in the timbered wall with the ladder against it, a matter of much speculation among the neighbours, and what looks like a weather-cock high on the roof.'

'At least it's not a T.V. aerial,' said our companion.

'They also commented on the fact that Noah had his animals driven into the building at night, which they saw as a senseless waste of time and fodder in that climate.'

'Here they are in their tiny craft, as it appears in the next picture, on the waste of waters, the outlook bleak and murky, the others on board beset by doubts. In their cramped and smelly quarters (while not strong on hygiene, the proximity of the beasts in the poorly ventilated barque kept stark reality before them) Noah's claim to have acted under divine guidance began to seem the vain boast of a senile old man.

That brings us to the heart of the story, the same that is at the centre of our private, personal ones. I mean the intimations that come at moments of crisis. After years of silent listening for signals coming from areas outside the circumscribed one of my mind, have some really reached me at certain times? Are they what impelled me to unreasonable risks and excesses, are they guiding us now?

'If Noah himself had lost faith, taken to his bunk and turned his face to the timbers, a shudder would have gone through the craft, the beasts would have ceased bellowing, grunting, mewing and squealing and have cowered silently in their slatted stalls.

'At that moment the ark would have crossed the meridian between myth and oblivion and have drifted out of all ken.'

FIVE

'I've an idea how to hoodwink old Liz!'

'Hoodwink?'

'Don't pretend you don't know what's in the air.'

There was no waiting for the spark to ignite in you. Before I could relate it to my seemingly unrealisable imaginings, you were planning a shopping expedition. You began reckoning how much money we could get together with what your mother had given me for a month's board and keep for you and the governess, plus what she'd entrusted to you.

'We'll have to buy stores.'

You drew up a list on which the amount of wine struck even me, and I'm a dedicated wine-drinker, as excessive.

'Leave it to me; I know what I'm doing.'

I left the wine to you but made some other reassessments.

You insisted on me coming with you to look for the aquarium that was high on the list. So I watched, somewhat detached, as the shop-man persuaded the girl and her parent (grandparent?) into buying a tank complete with an electrically operated shell that opened and closed at intervals, emitting a necklace of oxygen bubbles.

Next to the wine shop.

'Wine is what she can't resist after the first couple of glasses.'

I began to have a glimpse of a plan. Not a plan, for the dreaming semi-conscious cannot formulate anything so hard and fast, not to say cut and dried.

Was it she who was blamed for your disappearance after seeing the film in Lausanne as well as finally dismissed over the escapade here?

You nodded.

While Liz Considine was preparing our evening meal you helped me take the cartons of wine from the boot and stow them away above, not bringing more to the kitchen cupboard than might seem a modest supply for two people for two weeks, it being taken for granted (by whom?) that you wouldn't be drinking it with us.

One of the possibly irrelevant details I recall from those early days is how often, as we talked, you were leaning forwards—in this instance on your knees in the small loft storeroom—so that your remarks came through a gap in the curtain of hair.

'We'll try it out on her first and see the effect. The girls at school used to say they knew how many bottles she'd got through of an evening by the kind of daze she was in in class next morning and how long it lasted.'

Your governess was calling from the kitchen. Slip down the steep stair, being careful not to trip over the tabby on her way up, and answer from the garage where you were supposed to be getting things out of the car.

Liz Considine too had been doing some shopping, and with the slap-up meal seemed the time to bring out the wine and have the preliminary try-out. Preliminary to what, or, if it comes to that, try-out for what? I hadn't asked what you had in mind, nor you me; each had an instinct to leave it still nebulous.

I had to set the early pace but I soon saw that your suppositions about your governess's addiction had not been exaggerated. And between the two deep streams I noticed at least a trickle flowing to you.

You were humming some of the ballads sung in your English classes, evoking old times, and in a pause between two left the kitchen. When you'd been gone for I don't know was it two minutes or a quarter hour your governess called you and you sang back through the intervening doorways: 'The minstrel girl to the loo has gone.'

Your glance as you returned signalled: There you are, how's that for a start, what did I tell you! Just conscious enough to miss me from the table but in no condition to admonish, not even about not closing the bathroom door.

As you changed the plates you put a fresh bottle of wine on the table and I refilled the two glasses with a token drop in yours.

Herra: We won't be late.

Liz: That's a good girl.

Herra: Don't wait up; I'll slip into bed without waking you.

Liz: Not too late.

Herra (a lullaby): Not late, never late. . . .

You flitted about the shadowy part of the kitchen-dining-room which was lit only by the festive candles on the table, doing some washing up and telling your governess to stay where she was and relax after the wonderful meal she'd prepared. After the second of a couple of visits to the bedroom you emerged with what my alerted attention took in as an overnight case (I didn't care what it was called as long as I was sure what it meant) and went through in the direction of the garage. You came back and sat down again, lounging across the table with a marked lack of the decorum taught at the Swiss place, now evidently unmarked by its ex-mistress, and started a desultory conversation with Liz Considine in which her part was minimal.

I went to the car, leaving the disappearing act to be performed by you, which, as you reported, you managed so delicately that there was no jolt, jerk nor perceptible sense of severance.

There were some of the neighbours outside the cottages in the spring dusk and they averted their faces and fell silent as we passed. You opened your case and instead of the night attire I expected a glimpse of, there was this old steel helmet of the kind worn in the First World War, though by which armies I don't know.

'Let's pretend we're the Archduke Franz Ferdinand and his wife Sophie driving through the streets of Sarajevo.'

You caught up your hair on the top of your head and put the headgear over it. (Which were you, the Archduke or Archduchess?)

We were being driven away from the town hall in the Serbian city past the crowds, now silent and expectant after the first abortive bomb-throwing, Count Harrach crouched on the running-board with drawn sword, ready to defend the royal couple with his life. (Source: your school history books.)

'The fool of a chauffeur crawled along at a snail's pace.'

'I'm driving quite fast enough for these lanes.'

'The mood of the mob was less than loyal.'

We passed some youths out with a gun and a terrier about to blast the evening quiet, and you winced. On each side of the narrow road the dusk was gathering but not, I sensed, quickly enough for you, with the mysterious bond you had with the living shadows of timidity and fragility seeking its sanctuary.

'I got it in exchange for a bottle of cheap wine in the student's weinestube my mother had forbidden me to go to.'

I was getting used to your belated explanations and afterthoughts and didn't have to ask: 'Got what?'

You leaned back and took something else from your case, this time a scrap of printed paper torn from a news sheet.

'What a lovely countryside this is and what a Via Dolorosa for its creatures!'

You read out the letter to the newspaper in which a woman described what she'd seen at a coursing festival.

'In each of the two cases the hare was caught by both hounds, which engaged in a vigorous tug-of-war with their victim. This went on for two or three minutes, each dog pulling at the hare and the hare screaming all the time. One would then lose it but make another grab and sink its teeth into the mutilated body again, when the performance was repeated. They ran all round the field pulling and tugging. . . . In the other case the poor savaged body dropped to the ground and found the strength to hobble away from its torturers . . .'

Navigating three parts by instinct and one memory we reached a large, just about still-functioning hotel. An old gentleman and his daughter, pale-faced and, by the look of her, just into her teens (late second marriages sometimes turn out the best, but where's the mother?)

Is anything required before the bar closes? Before the drawbridge is lifted and the watchmen posted on the towers.

'I'd love an ice-cream.'

'Strawberry or vanilla, miss?'

'Could I have one of each?'

'If you'll kindly follow me, sir.'

What? Where? Oh, to show us the bathroom.

The porter, after guiding me down several passages and pointing to a door, returned to the ground-floor for our orders. I walked back what I hoped was the way I'd come, tapping on the doors when I thought I'd reached the point of departure.

Ah, Herra, don't vanish without a word like the leveret, or, less violently, while the intervals grew longer between her breaths until the final pause that has lasted ever since, a cat to whom I'd given (if that's the expression) my heart.

I recalled a solitude so intense it sucked in with the force of a vacuum unrealisable expectations, such as waiting for a car hired by you who didn't know of my existence, who perhaps wasn't yet born, to stop at the gate. Or when I lifted the receiver of the dumb instrument in case someone who hadn't the number was waiting to explain the long delay, and I heard the melancholy-sweet humming of my humming birds. When I finally found the room it was reunion again only a degree less miraculous than the first and second ones.

You were unpacking. Was this room yours or mine? I hadn't asked. You were taking one by one out of the small suitcase the objects at the top: the helmet, a missal, the newspaper cutting and the carton that had once contained a pair of Japanese binoculars and later the leveret for a few hours before we'd transferred it to the wooden, wire-covered box.

The porter brought the ice-cream, the bottle of wine

and some tomato sandwiches I didn't remember ordering.

'There's only one glass.'

'You can drink from mine.'

'And you can have some of the ice-cream.'

'It makes my teeth ache.'

'I'll warm it for you first.'

A pause, your mouth full. Then out came your tongue, blue from the wine you'd drunk earlier, with a melting blob of icecream sticking to it.

Herra, what behaviour!

What on earth do you think you're doing, girl?

If that's a game you played at the Swiss school . . .

A bit late for acting the serious, elderly companion across whose mind no thought of sex in your regard could pass.

I opened my mouth and took into it the double offering, warm and chilly, our tongues fused for about the second or two it had taken, looking over your shoulder that other night in the sitting room, for the meagre signs left there to produce the shock. What I suppose I'm suggesting is that having had the same nightmare together, it was natural, or, as they say in other contexts, inevitable, that we drew close in the other, prohibited, dream.

Later you said: 'I'll tell you about Lazarella, you remember her, not to try and get over it, which I don't want to do, but so that you too know as much about what happens to these creatures as you can bear.'

Why was she called Lazarella? Because she had risen from the dead and, having disappeared for three days, had slipped in through the window one blessed evening at dusk as you sat huddled over a book, but not really reading.

Then came the final disappearance, the days and nights of no resurrection, the final NOT.

You waited till dusk fell, with dusk came hope, though each evening less; it is then the silent shadows creep out of hiding places.

More than our tongues had touched. I knew the utterly solitary place where you'd been; it is where the theme for a novel is engendered, but also where thoughts of suicide can be encountered.

'I knew whatever I did: ringing the cats' home, advertising, making enquiries, praying, wasn't enough. I imagined Lazarella lost or trapped and still with a memory of me and that I would come to her rescue.'

You told me how when you returned to school you made the young maid promise to leave your window open and the bedside lamp burning at night; you couldn't bring yourself to confide your lingering hope to your mother.

Chased or strayed to a distant garden in a part of the suburbs that neither you nor she knew, thrown scraps by whoever happened to glimpse the bedraggled, exhausted creature, or somewhere else unimaginable: you had to try to imagine it, to try to share at least in thought in her agony. Rubbish dumps, ditches, drains, scrappily dug graves, holes in the ground.

The other image: the animal mask, furry mosaic of bright and dark, bronze and white, clear golden glance with the limpid reflection of a world that at moments you had entered.

Though your tongue had been loosened, as you put it, by touching mine, you weren't yet ready to tell me the end of the story. Not till a little later.

'What comes next?'

'You mean now.'

'Now and afterwards. Everything important that ever happened to me has been chance; unlucky chance like what I've been telling you or a lucky one like coming on that tour when it was Sweden we were supposed to be going to, only there was some hitch.'

'Isn't chance just another name for what we don't understand, like love?'

'It's easier to believe in a God of chance than a God of love.'

'There's a game we used to play with pieces of paper in the bath. I'll show it you if you've a pencil.'

Slips torn narrow, a near-sighted scribbling, pencil moving inside the tent of hair.

'Consulting the oracle, we called it. You write down the future as you'd like it, then as you'd hate it, as well as something in between. Whichever you draw out you don't have to keep to, of course, but if you're a believer in chance you're bound to take it seriously.'

'What are you putting down?'

'Housewife with town apartment and villa in country. And, number two, call girl.'

'Which category do they come under?'

'What?'

'Is either what you'd hate most or like best?'

'The housewife is the worst I can think of just now, and the other in between. The best is always the most difficult. You help me.'

'What do you hope for when you're alone, contemplative and at peace?'

'I'm never any of those things, except alone.'

'Can't think of anything.'

'The great imaginative writer! Oh, come on, its only a game.'

Is it? Was it? You'd the obstinate seriousness of the terrified child who will risk all in an attempt either to heal the wound or make it a mortal one.

You filled in the third slip, screwed it up like the others without letting me see it and said: 'Now lead the way.'

'Where?' Be precise; no evasions or ambiguities. Not that they were your weakness.

'The bathroom. Where did you think?'

Down the passages with never a light switch, or if there were any I couldn't find them.

An interlude while the hot tap was tested for its functioning (a sign that the ritual was more than a simple scattering of the lots on the water?).

'Give the cold tap half a turn, the other's scalding, and lock the door while I undress.'

'Which way?'

'Which way what?'

'Does the bloody thing turn.'

Don't ask which bloody thing. Don't say another word for a minute or two while I prepare for the shock of seeing you naked. 'Preparation' is only a manner of speaking and not a felicitous one at that. But I wanted to think about what was happening behind me (thoughtful by nature, with age I put thought before every step) and the why? and So what? and the Therefore of it. Putting to myself the questions, probably not the right ones, and the years between (mathematically, half-a-century) precluding my answers.

'I hope they're legible.'

'Legal?'

The roar from the taps made hearing difficult. And where were the heart-beats coming from?

You in bra and without knickers (hadn't been wearing

any? Discarded before the upper garment? What did I know of the habitual order?) showed up the low imaginative quality of my instant flights to sexy interiors.

'Try your wrist in it.'

I suppose I was so long in registering what you wanted that before I moved you had one foot in the tub. Then the other. And I saw the point of your order of undressing: bra, but not knickers, could be slipped off standing in the bath.

You let the scraps of screwed-up paper fall from your hand into the water. Then you squatted down gingerly, obscuring them and, I supposed, declaring the contest with fate, or however you saw the game, open.

'You should have thrown them over your shoulder,' I had the presence of mind to remark, showing I wasn't completely distracted from the ostensible matter in hand.

The pellet that I imagined was the one on which I didn't know what you had inscribed, possibly the expression of a hope in three of the most solemn words in the language (what words? A cry from the depths of isolation to somebody who at last seems within signalling distance) was floating just above your pubic hair.

You slid deeper into the water, lifting your arms and laying them along the rim of the tub to allow me as clear a field as possible. Should I shut my eyes before starting on the treasure hunt? Unnecessary, seeing that I had no reasonable means of distinguishing between the waterlogged scraps of paper.

Supposing . . . Supposing . . . that the quarry became one of the more responsive zones of your body. Might this be what you had in mind? No, not in mind; your mind, as I was slowly realising, was innocent of all duplicity. This was in my experience so unique that I was never reminded of it without a feeling of astonishment. In the inarticulate nerves, then.

'Let's have some more hot water.'

Straighten up—the ache in the lumbar region hadn't vanished under the rush of stresses from elsewhere—open the eyes, but no, they weren't closed, turn a tap, the wrong one.

'It started badly with the Sarajevo drive, but since then its been a blessed evening.'

Was it the first one you could have called that since the death of the leveret or even the disappearance of Lazarella?

Finding a soggy little ovoid—yes, I'd resumed the game—between my palm and your thigh, there was nothing for it but to retrieve it. Unscrew the disintegrating scrap of paper, *that* I could just manage, but read it without glasses, no.

'*You'll* have to read it, Herra.'

SIX

'Oh no. It's you who have to read it out and then let it go down the drain with the others.'

'Yes, I see.'

You were to face your God of Chance with me as referee. As I didn't know what was on the third lot, I couldn't cheat.

'Go and get them.'

I wiped my sweating face before unlocking the door.

'You've forgotten the slip.'

I picked up the spongy object from the floor and set off in the direction of your room. I hadn't memorised its number and once more I couldn't find it. I was reminded of a nocturnal journey I used to have to take as a child along a dark corridor and of the door, at about the half-way stage, that had been a friendly one. But now it was too late, by over fifty years, to tap on it. The occupant was gone, the house was gone, converted into a Government-run turkey-breeding establishment, and when I'd last looked for it there had been a notice on the gate: No entry on account of fowl pest!

A retreat back to bathroom.

'What does it say? Don't stand there looking like that and not telling me!'

'It says . . . I don't yet know what it says. I came back to see if you needed more hot water.'

One other guest or possibly a member of the staff was the only person I met in my continued search.

Stranger: Are you looking for . . .?

F.F.S.: It's all right.

Stranger: Can I . . .?

F.F.S.: I'm on my way to soap the missus in the bath.

I don't say the encounter took place, not on the factual level, but in my anxious imagination there were dozens of them.

On my final return to our bright and steamy bower there'd been a shift in the warm tide.

Instead of us taking the next step in elucidating the oracle, you were finishing telling me the story of Lazarella.

You had told the workmen clearing the stream that divided some of the suburban gardens to let you know if they happened to come on a ginger cat. A dead one, of course. And, oh yes, 'happened to.' There was—how well I know about that—a reluctance to mention the matter at all to them, and, forced to do so, a need to appear as uninvolved as possible. (You'd gone back a bit, having, in the earlier account reached the point of leaving for Switzerland.)

'They were soon bringing a lot of objects to show me, drowned, run over or mangled, I think, by dogs, not all of them even cats. They were all, or almost all, the colour of the filthy water. And there was one that just about could have been Lazarella.'

'I see.'

'Do you, though?'

'Partly.'

'Anyhow, you too can say: Better the leveret that vanished without trace.'

'Almost without trace.'

'Yes, just a tuft of speckled fur; defensive colouring, the thrush's breast is like that too, the beautiful, clean camouflage, and then this camouflage of filth and decomposition through which I couldn't recognise Lazarella.'

You were stretched in the bath, your arms still resting on the sides of the tub.

'Of course, I no longer expected a resurrection by then, just as Mary Magdalene didn't when she came running to the tomb. How close had they been, those two, what do you think?'

'I don't know.'

'He wasn't human if, when she was wrapping his feet in her hair and kissing them, the thought didn't occur to him. As I'm sure it occurred to you when you were taking the icecream off my tongue.'

I didn't say: I'm not Jesus and you're not Mary; no stupid or conventional remonstrance.

'Occur to me! It has obsessed me ever since and I've been trying to get it into manageable proportions.'

'Aren't you making a mountain out of a molehill?'

Was the transportation of this age-worn, thought-worn body-mind, imprisoned in drab masculinity, inside freshest girlhood's innermost femininity a molehill, a molehole?

'Let's have some more hot water for Christsake!'

As for Jesus, he knew what he was doing and not doing. As for me, almost any other girl would have done for that, were doing for it all the time, if not in my immediate vicinity. Where I wanted to be with you was in the world of grief and loss into which Lazarella hadn't been resurrected.

Mary. Herra. Woman-names spoken in desolate places, in a graveyard on an Easter morning, into an empty, humming telephone receiver on a winter evening.

You stepped out of the tub and were draped in a towel. What a nuzzable, suckable, lovable (on this level the adjectives roll off the tongue) delectable. . . . The unspoken litany was brought to an end by a rap on the door.

Had suspicion blown through the dark, upper floors after my meeting with the prowler there and reached the lower, managerial quarters from where a signal had gone out to the local gardai?

'What is it?'

'Is anything else required before we lock up?'

A signal to you not to ask for icecream, chocolate or vanilla.

'Nothing, thanks.'

Next morning on the homeward drive I told you about others in this mobile cell in which, alone or with a companion, so much had happened to me along wet and winding, or straight and heat-hazed, roads.

That incident that I had never thought I should confess: Driving back from my wife's funeral in my black suit and my face feeling set in its mask of non-feeling, this hitch-hiker held out her hand.

She slumped in the seat beside me in the same tired or indolent way she had signed to me to stop. The part of her I could see without taking my eyes off the road—I was driving too fast—was all thigh.

Let's see how she'd take it when I turned up a lane that obviously led nowhere and slowed down. She seemed to sink deeper into the seat and her knees went higher under the instrument panel.

'Did you feel bad about it afterwards?'

'It became clearer to me what sort of person I was at the lower levels.'

Driving through our parish village I slowed down for the family groups who were parading from their parked cars towards the church. You donned your helmet that you hadn't packed this time but had kept beside you.

'I wouldn't like to meet them on foot, alone, unsuitably dressed and going in the other direction.'

'One thing Jesus was spared, Herra, on his way to Calvary was an encounter with such a crowd of Sunday Mass-goers.'

It was I who knocked, not without some trepidation, on Liz Considine's door.

'*Herein!*'

So the watchdog was awake and thought it was you. I went in and there she was, still in bed, her face pale and blurred as though the hangover was contagious and I'd caught it just by looking at her. Or had it always been indistinct to me because of you, like a star too near the moon?

'I overslept; Herra should have wakened me.'

Ah, those mornings, which you don't know about, when one puts a brave face on it, pretending all is well, jumping out of bed and staggering at the impact of the floor that reverberates into the brain, advancing to the bathroom, slightly crouched for fear of hitting one's head on another of the obstructions that seem to be everywhere, for a sluice in water that's either too hot or too cold because giving the proper taps the correct amount of turn is beyond one. This woman was beset with all these miseries and, no doubt, others more specifically feminine. Though not, of course, by the familiar one of: Am I bloody pregnant? But others equally humiliating.

Not that, at one remove, this question hadn't plagued me too. I had sent a message to my love who'd returned to a distant city and had no telephone, or, if she had I didn't know the number. Nor had the Pill been thought of.

I tried various ways of putting it in the telegram. 'Could those couple of nights, not to mention the day between, have resulted in your becoming pregnant?' But though I altered the wording twice, three post offices refused it, saying it came under the prohibited category of offensive messages.

'You could have put it in German or French.'

'She didn't know a foreign language.' (This from a later conversation between you and me).

'Herra's preparing breakfast, and a large pot of tea, which will be ready as soon as you are, Mrs. Considine.' And, in answer to a look or a question: 'You didn't hear us go out, yes, we're early birds, at least we were this morning.' I didn't *say* we'd been to Mass, but the suggestion was there if she wanted something to reassure her.

Back in the kitchen you weren't preparing anything, just sitting at the table, chin in palms. I put on the kettle.

'When I told my mother that Lazarella had been found (though I wasn't quite certain the thing the men had shown me was what was left of her) she asked, only half attending: 'Is she all-right, darling?'

'That depends; she's dead,' I told her.

Liz, as I now began thinking of her though not quite yet calling her, came in and sat down, just about realising where she was, I imagined, and that she mustn't hold out her cup before I offered to pour out the tea.

Strike when the iron is hot, when the core has been softened and is malleable. 'I usually spend Sundays in my studio-loft and I'd like your and Herra's company.'

She was giving me what cloudy, headachey attention she could muster.

You had a paperback open before you on the table, to show, perhaps, you were less than whole-heartedly behind my idea of including your governess in our little community.

'What's palpable?' you asked. Even though you'd had breakfast at the hotel, it would have been better to have made a pretence of eating. I might have said: '*You* are.' And I'm sure Liz wouldn't have noticed anything, but I wasn't going to take that kind of cheap advantage of her. (Very praiseworthy, I hear you murmur.) But she hadn't drifted out of sight of land, our land.

'Please put away that book till after breakfast.'

She started to shake her head but quickly desisted.

'You'll join me then around midday when both of us will be more than ready, I daresay, for a pre-lunch aperitif.'

Yes, I imagined Liz reflecting, providing another half dozen cups of tea will see me through this desert between now and then.

You didn't like my suggestion. But how long did you suppose we could keep her in an alcoholic trance while we escaped into our private haven (ark, as you were already thinking of it)? There was another reason why I didn't want to try to abandon Liz. She was about the age that Nancy had died at; there were other similarities only recognisable by me. I couldn't ignore her welfare for the sake of what I thought was mine, as I had my wife's; I had a superstitious feeling that this was a second chance.

You appeared at the bottom of the ladder at the appointed hour but no Liz. When I asked you about her you shrugged your shoulders. Getting no answer to my knock, I entered the room and there she was lying on her bed with the coverlet over her eyes.

'I've got such a splitting headache I won't be going to Mass.'

Mass! An item long scrubbed from the agenda. She thought it was you: confusion number two.

'Mrs. Considine, or may I say Liz . . .?'

'Oh, it's you!'

'I looked in . . .'

'I don't know where it's leading.'

'Where what's leading?'

'You and she seem to understand each other so well. That can't be right with such a gap in your ages.'

'She had a desperate need for understanding when she tried to kill herself.'

'She told you about that?'

'No, but she will.'

'How can you be so sure? She wouldn't talk about it to our head mistress, nor to her mother. And, of course, not to me.'

'It's difficult to talk to others about states of mind they've never experienced. Though I'm not too sure about you, Liz.'

'Has that child been retailing school gossip?'

'"That child" doesn't have to tell me what I've an instinct for.'

'Yes, I've a hangover, if that's what you're getting at.'

'Listen, Liz; far from looking on hangovers as a shameful condition, I see them as one of the ways that people like us, not perhaps destined for the greater illuminations, gain some insights.'

No need to continue the verbatim report, is there? At which I can see you making one of your "faces".

'I'd love to hear,' you said (I'm putting it here, though that's obviously not where it fits in, so as not to forget it later), 'the other ways you tried wording the telegram.'

'Blanaid (her name came first in this one to help me get the message right, like holding her hand at a distance), are you sure, darling, we took the proper precautions?'

'That seems O.K. *I'd* have let it through.'

'What *wouldn't* you have let through?'

'Ah!' (End of interlude.)

'Do you know what, Liz; a severe hangover is a minor crucifixion. You're up on your cross in view of the respectable, wage-earning citizenry. Ever tried getting dressed on a cross? Of course you have, so have I. Or to put a sheet of paper in a typewriter on a cross, to say nothing of two, with a carbon in between.'

It was this last metaphor, of which I was quite proud, that I think got through and proved to her that I wasn't there as judge or, even worse, investigator.

'How are you feeling?'

'Terrible.'

I was by now sitting on your unmade, though unslept-in, bed, and Liz had risen slightly from the prone position, buoyed up perhaps by some of my words, her face unveiled, not to the brash day, but to the misty twilight I was evoking around us.

'It's someone on some kind of cross, no matter how deservedly, who can signal across to Herra on hers.'

'You haven't touched her?'

'She's just out of reach or I might have.' A prevarication? Not altogether.

I couldn't be more truthful until I had either decided she was too broken a woman in too precarious a position to make any final trouble, or, as I was beginning to believe, that she was another innocent victim.

'Do you know, Liz, there are children and adolescents in this holy land of ours for whom rape would be a lesser evil than constant exposure to the fact of small, helpless creatures, which their natural instinct is to cherish, being cruelly hunted and tortured while they have to learn to suppress their pity as a weakness?'

'You won't get round me with ideas like that; I've heard them all before.'

'What ideas, for God's sake?'

'Variations on the "make love not war" slogan.'

'No, not just with ideas, but I could have got round her easily enough by making love to her then and there.'

'How do you know?'

'By the signals.' Or, in plain poetry, by her not noticing that her breasts were half exposed (had I been wrong, she'd have pulled up the neck of her nightdress), and by her grey-green glance that rested on me in a kind of wonder half a second longer after each exchange of words than it would had the conversation absorbed all her attention.

'I began to guess what she'd been through and how her marriage had ended. It wasn't sex so much as insecurity and the fear of loneliness that impelled her, largely unconsciously, to be inviting.'

'How do you know so much about it?'

'From shameful observation of my wife, Nancy.'

'She thinks she's my guardian. Nobody guarded me from the real horrors.'

'She's had her share of horrors too, of a different kind.

The horrors that a disintegrating marriage inflicts on the partner who still clings to it and hopes against hope. That, as much as to act as your guardian, is what makes her afraid of being left out of it, of not being with us, and, of course, it's what made her start consoling herself on wine.'

'Didn't you want to?'

'I was too occupied with you. That's not to say I felt nothing. How should the old obsessive curiosity not have taken hold of me about what it would be like to move closer to her down the dark slope of sex?'

'I don't know why, but at times I'm convinced that nobody has so much to regret and to be sorry about as I have.' It's Liz again. 'Looking back on the last years of my marriage, that is. What made it all the worse was the memory of the earlier time.'

I glanced instinctively at the beginning of what I imagined as the big white, blue-veined breasts her husband had kissed and caressed and then later seemingly ceased to be aware of.

SEVEN

'There's a big, blue car at the gate!'

You burst into the room with the news that the look on your face was making your own sombre comment on.

And you didn't even know of the voluntary (as they'd called it) undertaking not to see you anymore while you were still under the legal age, and that I'm putting in my own illegal way. I'd signed it when I'd thought we'd seen the last of each other for at least that long, though I wasn't sure in months and years how many that might be.

'I wonder who it is,' trying to act unconcerned.

'The gang who came on Friday, that's who!'

Friday had it been? Then Good Friday had fallen on a Thursday this year.

'Were you expecting visitors?' asked Liz.

I heard the noise of a revved-up engine followed by the pause I recognised as indicating a change of gear from forward to reverse that was the welcome signal that somebody was merely turning their car in the gateway.

'Hurry and get the rest of what we need up to the loft,' you said when Liz was out of bed again and in the bathroom, 'being sick', you suggested. 'She used to have to leave the class room several times a morning after one of her booze-ups.'

Was it my attempt to persuade her that her nightmare world of hangover and counter-hangover, the desert with its poisoned oases, had, after all, been crossed by others and that she'd do better to keep company with explorers like myself, however suspect, than continue all alone her journeys into past and present ignominy? Or was it the promise of the aperitif? Anyhow, she appeared punctually at the foot of the ladder, accompanied by you.

The ascent was an ordeal and when she stopped half way up and raised her pallid face to me where I waited to give her a helping hand at the top, I interpreted the look as a distress signal such as the lost stragglers from migrating flocks send out on their sub-human wave lengths.

Settle the weary migrant who had only just made the coast with wings wet with salt spray ('trying to get me to open my heart to her', you called this kind of talk) on the couch and then get the cats. It was the last descent I intended making before evening when I expected Peter whose ties with me were not just those of blood but with whom I shared some unexpected thoughts. He was coming with a friend, a revolutionary from the North who, as Shakespeare put it: has a part i' the story, to take away the car. With it gone the place would appear deserted and the neighbours couldn't tell at night who had driven it away.

I had trouble enticing the two felines from the garden where these creatures of strictest habit were taking their midday prowl. When I had got them to the foot of the gangway-ladder, you with the tinkle of a spoon on a plate at the top attracted their attention. I could have caught and lifted them both in my arms and managed the balancing feat of climbing up and depositing them at your feet.

But I knew you wanted to see them ascend, one after the other, two small creatures only, and not even a mateable pair, but another of the means of keeping in touch with myth and guarding against the situation disintegrating into the commonplace or sordid.

I drew the curtains in the cottage and left on the light so that prying neighbours would suppose, when it got dark, that all was as usual and later when Peter and his revolutionary friend drove away in the Rolls (though the friend would in fact be driving the car they'd come in), after turning off the illumination, the same good Christians would suppose we had retreated.

Back in the loft, with gangplank drawn up and hatch battened down, I brought out the white wine and poured Liz and myself what in more formal times and circles was known as a generous measure. After she had had a couple of swallows I saw she was at the delicate balancing point between hangover and reintoxication, where, looking over the left shoulder, the shadows are murky, while over the right, the room begins to glow.

'It's begun,' you murmured, lifting your glass into which I had poured some token drops.

Yes, in our small and private manner we were reliving the original adventure in one of its many variations. The last train was moving out of the doomed city, the bird had flown from under the net of the fowler, the ark was lifting from the sodden earth.

How much was still for you a make-believe? Should I have told you then and there about the document I'd been persuaded to sign by what might or mightn't have been a trick, the sergeant, after being on the phone to the city, informing me that otherwise I'd be brought before the district justice and remanded?

Liz was our burden and blessing. Burden, because I was committed to imparting to her a feeling of being on the inner, instead of the outer, side of the communal door. Though there'd be plenty of wine, of an evening at least, bought with money your mother had provided for other, strictly defined, purposes, I'd abandoned the idea of keeping her in a state alternating between deep hangover and second or third degree drunkenness. A blessing, because she ensured our life would be orderly with the hours of your lessons as strong ribs in the structure of the day. Did you know that under the great pirate captains, Kidd and Morgan, discipline was as strict as on a man-o-war?

But on that first evening it was a mixture of alcohol and whatever you told her that made Liz agree to you both spending the night in the main part of the loft with me on my camp bed in the storeroom among the tins and bottles. Not that there was a discernible decision taken. It was a matter of you, on her last sleep-walking return from the bathroom, helping her into the bed that, as a couch by the table, she'd been floating on all evening.

We had to keep the place in semi-darkness if the vigilance of the neighbours wasn't to spot a glimmer from the skylight. The shaded lamp on the table left the rest of the loft, including the two beds, in shadow.

With your governess asleep and aswoon, the two cats curled on the empty bed, we held our breath. Or, if breathing, kept quite still, you stooped over a news clipping on the table, not sitting but bent right over, your head in your hands that were under your falling hair.

'You must know it by heart.'

'"Only eight hares died in fifty-two courses". They print the number every day.'

'And you make yourself read and memorise the reports.'

'Look!'

You stood up straight and held out your hands. For me to take? To show me your wrists.

Where two blue veins converged closest before diverging and disappearing into the whiteness of your inner arm they were crossed by red threads with darker pinpricks on either side made by the stitches. The wounds looked fresher and more inflamed than when I had first noticed them.

'There's where it pains.'

There was a sentence in a book on biology that I'd read and, without fully understanding, remembered: 'The same code of triplets of bases is used to define the proteins in all organisms; we're all one flesh.'

'Sometimes they open and suppurate.'

'Are you going to bed now?'

'Can I have the aquarium beside me for company?'

I shifted the tank to the table and retired to my bright cubby hole (it had no skylight) to let you undress.

Once open the door into the house of no clocks and perpetual twilight, and appointments made elsewhere will scarcely be observed punctually. I opened a book and John Lodwick, years dead in a car crash in Spain, was speaking to me again through a passage in his last novel; did you think I wasn't coming back?

But you'd been enclosed in another world too, cool, dim, aquatic, arranging your treasured odds and ends in the aquarium. Your bare arms, luckily you had on a sleeveless nightdress, were up to the elbows in the water, your fingers and the fish gleaming in the light from the table-lamp as you constructed a golden arch with one of your bracelets. And draped over one of the miniature rocks, that, with the electrically-operated shell, formed part of the original decor, were the onyx cuff-links I'd missed at your mother's.

From Liz's bed muffled echoes from the depths of unconsciousness.

'Let's have a look at your wrists.'

'Just a minute; lend me your watch.'

With the granite slabs, it was my only memorial to a past I set such store on. I took it off and gave it you.

From somewhere (a secret recess of your handbag?) you produced the type of contraceptive known as a French letter and unwound it over the watch, tying the end with thread. Then you lowered this new contraption into your water garden so that the watch rested, dial upwards, among the water plants.

By now your hands were blue and when I took them in mine, instead of warming them, my own became cold.

'Not like that.'

You took one of my hands and drew it under the bed clothes.

'It's a small wild animal that's slipped in and is hiding there.'

All right; relax and let it be guided by yours. Don't try to distinguish the precise location of the nest where you placed it.

A pause, and now I really held my breath.

Which, of course, you noticed. 'It's lying so still as if afraid to breathe, perhaps it doesn't like the smell of soap.'

'Herra, this is too serious to turn into a game.'

'I know that, I'm not a child, or I don't feel like one when I start thinking as I did to-night, when you were so long coming back, about death.'

'What do you think about it?'

'That it's too awful to mention when someone is very ill or in danger, whether a human or animal. When Lazarella was sick once with the shine gone out of her eyes I did all I could to try to keep that word away. So how can I bear the shock of hearing of people who, instead of protecting wild and frightened creatures in their power, watch one after another being torn apart for sport? Is it any wonder the cuts on my wrists open again?'

You were exerting once more an almost imperceptible pressure on my hand that I neither withdrew nor, as far as I could tell, let move of its own accord.

It was our first exploratory walk in our Garden of Eden, that you'd perhaps been prefiguring with your water garden; it was the small, wild beast you'd already mentioned brushing you with a healing, electric touch. It was a universe away from the world of the pornographers. Your fantasies, neurotic ones by general (that's to say, corrupt) standards, created their own ethic.

When I withdrew my hand I looked at it to make sure it was the old, ink-stained, earth-stained, familiar one; I even sniffed it and from the fingers breathed in a scent that brings all arguments and most conversations to an end.

'Wafted across a battlefield it would make the combatants throw down their weapons.'

'Think of the wild creatures seeking each other from far when they scent it on the wind.'

May the blessing of the condemned be with you. Peace to you both in your wilderness. Who, for God's sake, was this? And where was I? Lying beside you.

'Hush.' Had I spoken? 'You've been dreaming.' I, who never dreamed apart from the half-waking, self-conducted sex tours? Was I not in the garage, and had the messenger not come for the car? Or was I lying in Ophelia's bandaged arms, except that they hadn't needed bandaging? 'Lady, shall I lie in your lap?' (Hamlet.)

Gently, without signs of haste, to let you know, in the language of mime, that all this had been arranged and foreseen, free myself from your semi-embrace (if that's what it was, how, in the full one preserve the rational faculties intact?) and lift the trap door.

The second of the up-turned faces I recognised as that of Mullen, the guerrilla leader, or if that description implied a knowledge I didn't then possess, let's say: the revolutionary.

In my socks I let myself down onto the roof of the car, already pock-marked with the droppings of the house martins that had built in the rafters, and, via the long, shiny top of the bonnet, onto the floor of the garage.

'Thanks for showing up so punctually (not that I'd an idea of the hour); care to come in?'

'You mean up?' asked Peter.

'They're asleep up there.'

'So we're not to meet the problem child?'

'Why do you call her that?'

'I was only repeating what I read in the Sunday paper.'

'Don't say there've been stories!'

'That she sought asylum here because in the Calvinist school there weren't proper facilities for attending Mass.'

'For sweet Christ's sake!'

'Don't let it trouble you, Mr. Sugrue,' said Mullen, 'we've come here with a suggestion.'

'*He* has,' corrected Peter. 'I'm here to fetch the Rolls and, if convenient, to meet Miss Friedlander.'

Another touch of the facetious to remind me that it

was inhospitable (blood is both thicker, and a better medium for the relaying of signs and signals, than water) to keep them here in the draught.

'Just a minute; I'll see if you can come up.'

I climbed back, pleased at the feat at my age, which you didn't take in.

'We won't linger,' one of them, Peter it sounded like, called.

Back at your bed I asked: 'Shall I bring them up, they've something or other to discuss?'

'I don't mind coming down.'

'One of them is a stranger.'

'Can I keep on my nightie, it does as a summer dress?'

'Put something over it.'

'We're coming up. O.K.?'

Peter was getting impatient.

'No, we'll be down in a minute.'

'What about Liz?' I was uneasy.

'She's fast asleep.'

I went over and regarded her. Oblivious rather than sleeping soundly. She was one of those always deceived, whether in marriage or other relationships. I was the latest in the succession of betrayers, whether minor, as her pupils, or the kissing-Judases.

An episode of the story of the Good Samaritan that Christ hadn't had the heart to include: The first to pass by, even before the priest, one who hadn't crossed to the other side because it was on this side he had made the rendezvous he was keeping, was Fintan F. Sugrue. He had taken the battered, recumbent body and moved it a little further into the ditch, thus clearing the path and obviating any delays or hitches when his eagerly-awaited companion put in an appearance.

No response and I left it at that.

'What sort of stranger?' you asked.

'What kind of . . .? A Samaritan, wasn't it?' I'd been too deep in my sense of guilt to realise at once who you were talking of.

'Oh, Mullen; a quite ruthless individual, by all accounts, with primitive tastes in food, reading and, so they say, no interest in women, though he's married with several children.'

'I'd like to meet him.'

No cause to complain at your eagerness; I'd fallen to sleep and had even been dreaming.

'We'll lower the ladder.'

I wanted you to make a decorous appearance, and besides I was bringing down a bottle of wine.

If I hadn't had you with me, I too might have left a sufficient sum to defray all expenses.

'She's breathing funny.'

'She's all right.'

It wasn't the time for her to be anything else. If I took note of every nervous remark of yours on top of my own tendency to interpret the unusual in the most unfavourable light (this sort of snoring-breathing might be termed unusual or untoward) then we were sunk before we'd properly set out.

'Better breathe funny than not at all.'

Make light of it; concentrate on getting you down suitably attired (what was suitable in the circumstances?) and in a calm state of mind.

It went decorously enough; your bottom descending in front of the rest of you didn't look as if you were flaunting it or in any way conscious of, let alone exulting in (how weak was still my faith), a precocious dominance over the old man.

I kept the introductions formal, repeating Miss and Mister before, betwixt and behind; none of the 'Here's Herra, Peter; Hello Herra, this is John, hello' kind of casualness. Let it be sober-side upwards to start with; I was listening to hear if the heavy breathing from above was audible.

Once settled in the car with the bottle of German wine and the glasses which I'd insisted on bringing in spite of your saying they weren't required, I saw you were going to be all right. Really all right, not has-to-be all right, like poor Liz.

Mullen was talking to you as if he knew you far better than from the picture of 'the problem child' or the still more astonishing one of the devotée seeking religious asylum that he might have got from the papers.

He was telling you, rather than me, about the ghetto that he and his friends had chosen, or been forced, to occupy in the northern town whose name you'd never heard.

'There must be something that keeps you so united.'

This was just the company for you; how could I have thought otherwise?

'You'd have to know a bit of our history to grasp the deep division between them and us.'

'Oh, I know it without history, though it may not be the same "them" that I have to deal with as best I can.'

'Our enemies are national ones, Miss Friedlander, those who are fascinated by the golden age of utilitarianism where things are valued by their power to make life easy, pleasant and purposeless.'

I was listening to Mullen with a mixture of respect and distrust.

'Once, long ago, our missionaries pushed back the frontiers of barbarism on the mainland of Europe, at least it was a human barbarism, now we're up against a mighty machine.'

'Shit!' commented Peter.

'I apologise on my friend's behalf for that word.'

'Oh, it's not words I'm afraid of.'

Mullen went on to tell you about the barricaded, no-go area of the town run by the guerrillas.

'There's more real living, by which I mean fraternity, in the ruined streets than down in the centrally heated villas.'

You were already half won over; Peter, who'd been there, saw it as a ghetto of religious orthodoxy over which Mullen exerted his personal power. As for me, I wondered was this a solution to our immediate problem.

'You've guessed why I'm here, Mr. Sugrue?'

'Well. . . .'

'On behalf of the Committee of Five I invite you to the Laggan where you can do your own work, of course, while helping us run a centre which we're calling a Hall of Fraternity.'

'What about me?'

'You're welcome too, Miss Friedlander. All the more so as I understand it was to be able to practise your religion freely that you absconded from your Calvinist school.'

Christ Almighty! I managed to give you a surreptitious dig meaning: Keep your mouth shut.

'There's work for you too, if only getting the hordes of stone-throwing kids and stray animals off the streets.'

The mention of the animals clinched it.

'Couldn't we?'

'Couldn't we what?'

'She means: couldn't you both return there with me,' Mullen said, as if I didn't know what you meant! Then why ask? I hear you murmur, and, of course, you're right.

'How long did you plan to hide up there?' Peter made an inclination with his head toward the loft. Though it was me he asked, he followed the question with a look at you who were opposite (Mullen, you and I on the back seat, he on one of the occasional ones), the first attentive scrutiny he'd made of you.

'Why do you ask?' One thing about blood kinship, it cuts out the need for the round-about.

'They'll find you if you drag it out too long.'

He'd always been what's called a realist, the bringer of chill tidings to me the besieged, or the prisoner-on-remand or, more fancifully perhaps, the lost, and foolhardy, explorer. Though you, as a habitual mythologist don't care for metaphors and won't like these.

This was the moment to drink up the wine in our glasses. Not much, a bottle between four, but there are moments of decision and crisis when even a glass helps. It's a matter of performing a small customary or hallowed ritual, letting a physical act, however limited, interrupt the mental onslaught. Perhaps the drinking of a tumbler of water would have the same effect.

Peter read the papers, listened to the news on the radio (there wasn't, naturally, a television set on his fishing boat). He even had acquaintances in unexpected quarters, among those whom we, and Mullen, thought of as 'them'. What he'd just said about 'them' eventually finding us indicated that there were facts that I wasn't aware of. As usual, once alerted to what I had been optimistically ignoring the possibility of, I went to what might be another extreme.

I was suddenly receiving signals from one of those outpost nerves, that had till a moment ago evidently been asleep on sentry-duty, about your mother. How far was she to be trusted? If I was being kept under surveillance, or rather if they failed in this, would a search be instituted, with her approval, or even at her instigation, for us both? Had she only now, since her return home, finished my novel and realised what it was about and the sort of person who must have written it? Her original enthusiasm had probably been a misunderstanding arising from first having read the sympathetic postscript by the American professor and then given a cursory glance at the thing itself.

As you know very well, Herra, where I'm most vulnerable is in my imagination, as you are in yours, which illuminates a fictional world, as yours does the animal kingdom. And as happens to you, most of the arrows of my misfortune penetrate through this slit in my defences. So, if the hunt for us was on, I saw it as impelled, if indirectly, by hostility to my novels.

'What you don't realise, Pete, is that a move just now would disrupt the way of life we've just started on after all sorts of difficulties and setbacks, some of which you don't dream of.'

'Perhaps I do. But a move needn't disrupt anything.'

'It's all right for you, you're like the snail and carry your shell with you.'

'How does he manage that?' you asked.

'I catch herrings and mackerel.'

'Oh! With a boat?'

'Right, darling!'

He had taken his look at you, accepted you into the fold (it was not identical with ours) and from now on would talk to you, shout at you on occasion and give you a rough cuddle. I mean without the reserve that something excessive in him (we weren't close relations for nothing) made necessary with most people.

'Could you take us on it?'

It never rains but it pours. No, I won't forgo the old sayings where I can fit them in. I love them, even if you don't. How many wonderful possibilities suddenly loomed up before you!

'Not Fintan. We decided against the two of us going into partnership long ago soon after Nancy's (why, I wondered in passing, call her that instead of by the term for the kinship between them) death. But you can come anytime, Herra.'

Was he serious, you asked me with a look.

Yes and no. The idea of sailing to the North-West fishing grounds with you as his girl obviously fascinated him and you were going to have the central role in some of his future fantasies (a deep-sea fisherman, like a sailor, must depend a lot on these). Having what I knew could be called a healthy sexual appetite, this swift figurative, very figurative, ha, ha! (don't wince!) signing-on of you by Pete conferred on you right away the status of real womanhood that a computer, programmed with mere temporal data, wouldn't have come up with.

Perhaps the mention of a fishing trip, which Mullen took in his own quite different, serious way, made him hasten with his proposal.

'The Committee of Five (it sounded as if he was giving it capitals) have authorised me . . .' We'll skip the solemnities with which small dissident bands, guerrillas and such, try to factualise, or realise, their alternative, dream world over against the big, established, but also largely dream, one.

They needed someone to widen their image (his expression) and help them with their communications and manifestos (my interpretation). Why me? Because somebody or other up there in what was known as the Laggan had read some of my novels and deduced, with surprising insight, from those utterly non-political pieces of fiction attitudes not unconnected with theirs.

Prepare yourself for a shock, darling. Why the sudden 'darling?' Because even the memory of that hour or two with the two men in the car and you in the middle sends a chain-reaction of subtle but intense explosions from the brain through nerves and glandular organs.

Not, of course, that you don't know what's coming, but it sounded so fantastic at the time that it's bound to keep a trace of surprise.

'We would leave you your own small territory of freedom within the larger area of liberation where you could do as you saw fit. Officially we would appoint you as station-master.'

Before I could think of a comment, Pete came in with: 'The Chinese version, meaning Honorable Controller of Provincial Traffic, was one of the oldest and most respected titles in that country in days gone by, and possibly still is under Chairman Mao.'

Was this a piece of the humour that makes a slow start but by degrees reveals, in comic strip-tease, hidden zones of hilarity? Would the four of us shortly to be doubled up with laughter?

But Mullen was in deadly earnest. Humour doesn't thrive at the high altitude of icy gleams and black shadows where he was. It's much the same, as I well know, when the imagination is focused on sex to the exclusion of all else, or, if you like, on various forms of torture and execution. Graffitti are seldom consciously funny and the easy laugh is only heard when the sensual and psychic pressures are down at the lower end of the scale.

Of the four of us, as you soon sensed, Peter was the only one who took a cool look at everything under the sun.

The disused station, Mullen explained, would be the first public place on this island where there'd be a chance to experiment with what, as it became the commonest subject for argument in the conversations of the socially-minded, for all practical purposes was a pious myth.

'I'm talking about freedom.'

It was this occasional lapse of Mullen's into a dismal portentousness that I didn't like.

'You don't say,' remarked Peter. 'He's opening a fish-and-chip shop in the ghetto, and for a moment I thought he was going to make Fintan manager of that.'

I'd read in the papers, which you hadn't, that Mullen owned a chain of these places, which I only mention in passing as a possible reason for the initial association between him and Peter.

'I don't know that I've understood where I come in.'

Nor had I. The obscurity to which I was accustomed made it hard for me to realise that somebody (Peter?) had mentioned me to Mullen and his revolutionary friends when the strange idea had occurred to them to put someone in charge of their project outside their own ranks.

'Imaginative thinking, that's where. You can rethink the old assumptions about what constitutes freedom and fraternity, show us how to remove the by-now almost immovable walls we've built around each small group of us.'

This touched you; you exclaimed, in spite of your shyness in company: 'Yes, it's our separation from each other that's so terrible. We're shut up in our cells and don't hear the screams of terror coming from next door.'

'We're doing our best to force open some of the doors,' Mullen told you.

'It's not just the walls between us humans; we're indifferent to what's going on out there: we can't hear it. Listen!'

You held up a hand under the dim glow from the car ceiling-light, whether to indicate the dark countryside or to ask for silence, wasn't certain. For a moment I even supposed you might have heard a car stop or footsteps on the gravel.

'Nothing; the walls are too thick. But they're there, lying wounded where they've crawled into the hedges, dying in all sorts of ways, from gunshot, in traps and snares and, also, for entertainment, torn to pieces by dogs.'

I took the hand you'd let drop back on your lap. But I wasn't going to try to stop you in spite of a look from Mullen that I took as indicating that I should.

'What's it matter, a few of them less, who cares? That's what they think. But what happens here to-night and to-morrow is part of what happened somewhere else a long time ago. If we think it isn't, that's part of the separation and isolation of everything that we've invented. It means that Christ didn't rise after all, that his body rotted in a ditch or was eaten by dogs like the hares. God sent him to speak to us and that's what was done to him, so perhaps God tried again and sent the weakest, most innocent creatures to speak in an even simpler language.'

You were trembling, or, more precisely, long sighs were being followed by suppressed sobs with some swallows between as you tried to hide your face against me.

Mullen looked puzzled, neither your Christ nor the animals had, I guessed, much relevance for him. Peter leant forward and touched your head in a gesture I hadn't thought him capable of.

'Poor child!'

He had long ago come to the same conclusion as you, though for quite different reasons.

EIGHT

They were gone, Peter in the ancient chariot that he was taking to a shed he had in the fishing port where he kept his trawler and Mullen to the city, after promising to be in touch with me soon to hear my decision about the job. Up in the loft it was the deepest hour of night, our hour, the one we'd been secretly weaving during the last part of the too-prolonged visit and now gathered round us. The hour, you said, when the nuns in the convent that had been your last but one school rose to say one of the night offices.

'Ah.'

What was coming now? But I saw you had the missal in your hand that I'd noticed somewhere before, perhaps in the car the day Liz had insisted on my driving you and her to Mass.

You opened it and showed me a page of psalms in three columns, Latin, German and English (the convent, whose mother house was in America, was in a castle on a Bavarian lake) and these were split into short passages by a thin red, dividing line. You explained that the nuns in stalls on opposite sides of the choir intoned them alternately.

'I see.'

'You'd sooner we didn't pray?'

'Not if it makes you calmer. Show me your wrists.'

But you hid them behind your back.

We sat on your bed and reading from the same page I began with: '*Benedicto, Noctem quietam et finem perfectum concedat nobis Dominus omnipotus.*'

Silence, except for Liz's breathing.

'That's where you say Amen,' I reminded you.

'Did I sound like a hysterical kid who wants to be noticed?'

'I don't know how you sounded to Mullen; not to Peter and me.'

'Let's try the English.' You were letting my tongue, that had once touched yours, off its struggle with the unfamiliar sounds.

'They gaped upon me with their mouths, as a ravening and a roaring lion.'

I came in with: 'I am poured out like water and all my bones are out of joint . . .'

'For dogs have encompassed me. . . . they pierced my hands and feet.'

Liz sat up in bed and, her eyes still closed, exclaimed: 'God, Oh God!'

You went and put an arm around her shoulder.

'I must . . . I have to . . .'

'What? Spend a penny, or let's say tuppence?'

She opened her eyes at your voice but didn't answer, didn't see you, didn't see me, lay back again and started a faint moaning that was not unfamiliar to me and that, in my case, would have meant: Onto what blasted heath have I wandered or been taken from that other, earlier-evening venue, filled not with wild song and dance, nor any abandoned revelry for which this might be fitting punishment, but with quiet voices merged in deep discussion to which I was contributing ever profounder insights?

On your return to our side of the choir-loft your brief conventual mood, if that's what it was, had been dispersed. You took the missal from me and placed it, not among the other memorials in your water garden as for a moment I thought you were going to, but on the table beside the aquarium.

'I wouldn't have created a scene like that if I'd had time to come to myself before they arrived.'

'You didn't create a scene, at most a slight surprise, more a diversion from Peter's mockery of Mullen's brand of revolution. But I thought you'd been awake before they came.'

'Only a moment or two after one of those dreams.'

'Tell me.' Here, as with Liz's symptoms a moment ago, I wasn't on unsure ground.

'You know it all.'

'Yes, but let's share it again.'

'In detail?'

'In detail.'

'In a big building, all stone passages and vaults and halls, that's where I was this time, trying to find a way out, with a parcel, a loosely-wrapped, brown-paper bundle in my arms. In it was the mangled remains of a creature that I was trying to keep together so that its nearly-severed head didn't tear loose from the body and the broken legs didn't dangle from the parcel.

'I was looking for somewhere to bury it, walking up and down the corridors, being directed to a fire-escape I couldn't find, feeling a movement under the wet paper like the twist in your arms a cat makes to free itself when you're carrying it where it doesn't want to go.'

The hour when the Great Silence is broken in enclosed monasteries for Matins, or is it Compline, when the last, or last-but-one drink is being drunk before the party is over, when, on the way home from the pub, pockets are searched and wallets opened to try to calculate how much of the week's wages have been squandered on what will become a week's regret, when the would-be lover slips down a passage and knocks twice on a door, the hour, perhaps, when Noah heard a woman's shrill cry break the silence to enquire if he really knew whose voice it was he had claimed was giving him instructions these last months.

Before I could suggest you going back to bed I saw your practised hand, practised at minute adjustments, re-arranging or transforming the water garden into one more evocative of the counter-dream, the one, I guessed, of forests and jungles where man and his machines were unknown.

I went and washed my face and rinsed out my mouth in the tiny wash room; one of my ways of coming to a halt on a steep decline as yours had been the saying of the psalms. When I returned you were stretched on your back on the bed, your long, pale legs like the stalks of some early garden delicacy just pulled from the earth.

'Listen,' you told me.

A faint plop, plop.

'That's the fish; it's the time of night they start feeding if there's anything floating about.' One of the many smaller events I'd left out of my nocturnal time-table.

I was at the bed, trying to get a look at your wrists.

'They're O.K. Isn't that what you were going to drag up?'

'Good-night, Herra.'

You raised your arms and I let myself be pulled onto you. But in an attempt to control myself I tried to imagine I was being lifted onto a mortuary slab and that what was happening to me physically was rigor mortis setting in.

'Don't treat me like a child!'

That's all I needed. Nothing that feeds the healthy imagination need be taboo. Who said that? Catching sight of a peasant skirt in the yard of a winter evening, Squire Tolstoy had only to whistle and the woman came without a word, whether she was thirteen or forty. What for mauled Christ's sake had this to do with plain bloody F. F. Sugrue at this probably fateful moment in the latter part of his varied existence? What had the Count and his big-bottomed Matrushka, not to mention the horse-hair sofa, to do with here-and-now, you and me?

I was a coiled cone, a rocket ready to be released.

'Don't worry; I'm not a virgin.'

An upward glance from you that I interpreted as: Let him find out if that's true in the only way that's left.

No, not just a child in the low-teenage bracket, to use technical jargon. Or only by the time-table. Emotionally, psychically far advanced, mentally erratic, sometimes maddening but also far from common immaturity, magnetic (what's that?) and the victim of intense and detailed obsessions.

'Oh!' Which of us was that?

The tender, just-dug-up, mouth-watering-inducing stalks were curling round me. The watch face gleamed pale in the under-water jungle. The cross on the cover of the missal was the meeting-point of the painful recent past and the fragile future.

One of your cold, again-wet hands was on the back of

my neck pressing my face towards yours with the same gentle, agonised pressure that I imagined you exerting in the dream to keep the parcel together. I reached back and detached it, taking it in mine finger by finger.

'This little fish went to market,
this one got wet,
this one's a pearl from the bed of the sea
and this little fish my love gave to me . . .'

You couldn't help it, you burst out laughing, though you were also frowning at the possibility that I was evading the vital issue.

A knock from below on the trap door.

'There wasn't!' I can hear you exclaim indignantly. 'None of your novelistic tricks!' No tampering with our private scriptures!

No, nothing happened to interrupt us; so I had to continue leading you, finger by finger, away from the brink over which I'd been ready to plunge with you. (I'm constantly aware of your possible comments, such as: pseudo-romantic!)

'You don't want it with me, do you? Say the tender truth. Not enough of a woman, am I? Just a half-crazed, immature kid who can't give you a . . .'

I slapped my hand over your mouth to stop you saying the word that would have undone all I'd been doing by reasoning with myself.

I got up from where I'd been lying, in shirt and trousers, yes, but, also yes, between your tendrilly tender legs.

Oh, tenderness was suddenly there in plenty just when I'd made myself face the 'fact' that I was carrying on like a bull!

'We weren't approaching it from the right direction, Herra.'

'What direction is that, for the love of God?'

'The one we should come to everything important from, our mythology of love and pain.'

'You mean, like the ice-cream kisses, when I pretended my tongue had been loosed by touching yours so that I could tell you about Lazarella?'

'Imagining isn't pretending.'

'I'm hungry.'

As you got off the bed I saw that under the nightdress you still wore the knickers that, with the jeans, you'd pulled on at the arrival of the visitors. The brink might have been further off than I'd supposed.

'I'm going to make sandwiches,' you called from the cubby-hole of a kitchen.

I sometimes think our time in the loft could best be evoked in a play, not necessarily for public performance, even a mime. Then there'd be dialogue and/or the dance, and directions such as, at this point: F. crosses, right, to Liz, and stands by her cot regarding her anxiously.

Had she opened her eyes and, this time, seen us and quickly closed them again to shut out the sight of your destruction that must have seemed part of the visions of horror that flashed through her drunken slumber?

NINE

We were back on your bed, eating the so-called sandwiches that you'd made by balancing tomatoes sliced in half on pieces of thickly-buttered bread.

'I see I've a lot to learn.'

'What are you thinking of in particular?'

'The sex dream.'

As usual your instinct was true. You'd given yourself time to sort things out in the kitchen and realised that the direct, factual approach wouldn't do for you, for me, for us. Which was what I'd suggested, hadn't I, before you'd retired there.

A squelching sound (quite appealing!) as you sucked up a piece of tomato from a slice of bread.

'I'm not in your dream.'

'If you only knew!'

'Oh, don't pretend. What you were going to give me, before finding you couldn't go through with it, was a practical lesson in biology.'

'Sweet Jesus!'

'You didn't even kiss me.'

'Once get my mouth on yours and the other horn of the ravening beast would have found its way into the even more vulnerable and ancient wound, the one that opened in flesh long, long ago before human mouths were dreamed of.'

'Ah,' you murmured, touched, as I'd hoped, by the legendary slant, 'tell me.'

'What?'

'About what you call the ancient wound and how it happened.'

Hardly a modest (I don't mean morally) request.

'Where shall I start?'

'At school it was with the fishes.'

'Fine! Here goes (the latter exclamation was made more to myself than to you to rally my powers of improvisation, which, incidentally, are quite considerable).

'What made the first amphibians, why did the fish-reptiles, emerge from the ocean?'

'Don't ask me.'

'I'm not. I'm looking for the right rhythm. Ever hear the saying once fashionable in literary circles: Hit on the style and you've found the story? Anyhow: they were impelled by a dream, an obsession about, an urge towards, something still inconceivable in fish or reptiles; a localised bulge. And at last the marine fantasy became flesh, a mammal appeared, as the creator, or developer, pronounced another of his *fiats*: Let there be paps!'

'Eh?'

I touched one of yours through the nightdress.

'Go on.'

Doing what? It had to be telling the legend.

'There came a moment on the warm sands when the longed-for penetrability of female flesh was no longer a joke or a fantasy, and a sick one at that, very possibly, to certain conservative marine creatures, but fact, fact, fact!'

'Why could it only happen on dry land?'

'Ever tried suckling an infant under water? The rare liquids and lubricants essential to sensuality can only be secreted in areas of comparative dryness.'

A tomato slice toppled from the slippery surface of the piece of bread I was holding and you caught it. I bent and ate it out of your palm, leaving a little residue of pink juice and saliva.

With the sandwiches you'd brought an opened tin for the cats and, scenting the unscheduled repast, they left Liz's bed and padded over to us. You still held your hand with the drops of dew in it cupped.

'Why did you have them neutered?'

Oh, it wasn't the time for explaining the practical view about two female felines in a cottage besieged by hungry toms. Not when we'd just reached the mammalian paps and moist entries and exits. (Exits? There's been nothing about exits, you'd have objected with your insistence on detailed clarity if I'd put it like this at the time.)

'Tell me.'

'Why I had them spayed?'

'No, no! About the voice out of the void pronouncing the *fiat* (what an ad. they could have made of it if there'd been cars in those days!) to let there be life.'

I hadn't quite caught up; you went on: 'If the earth trembles at every copulation what must it do when a woman conceives?'

'Who says it trembles?'

'Don't say it doesn't, or that nothing happens, or I'll feel as let down as when I found out about Santa Claus.'

Which couldn't have been so very long ago.

'It's a secret event without, at first, any outward signs or portents.'

'Describe it, the secret, make it sound fabulous.'

Challenged like that, as at times in my fiction, I had to be inspired.

'The millions of spermatozoa are wriggling their way towards where the mythological "let there be life" is uttered over one of them.'

'Which one? What decides?'

'Any one, apparently. We're back to your god of chance.'

'You've begun half-way through. Where did they come from?'

'The male sperm?' Your eyes were never dark except when you were listening intently. 'It's like the sudden rush of sparks up a chimney when a smouldering log is stirred.'

'The log being the penis?'

'Symbolically speaking.'

'All right.'

'They're almost all tail and nearly transparent and they soon burn out and vanish in the dark, all except the one that hooks on to a different kind of cell, the female one, deep up the tunnel.'

I caught deep breaths and then didn't as if you were holding them.

'The couple involved know nothing about it.'

'*I* would.'

The cats licking their paws and passing them over their whiskers with the peaceful, age-old gesture that Herod and Cleopatra must have seen in the midst of their disorderly lives.

'Shall I ever have the chance?'

'Why not, it's up to you.'

'I'm not sexually attractive, am I? From you I expect the truth as well as all the other things, and you know I can face worse realities.'

'I've told you and you won't listen.'

'You couldn't go through with it just now, that's what I felt, no matter what you said. It could be because you're too old and, if so, you must tell me that too. But I think it's because I'm not very exciting.'

'Herra.'

Your face paled as it would had it been slapped and before it had time to redden.

'Pain, yours or mine, mustn't stop you.'

'You ask if I'm too old, meaning physically, and the answer, as they say in the council halls, is in the bloody negative. But old men, according to the poet, Yeats, and other lesser authorities, have strange obsessions. There are cases, like that of King Leopold the first, king of the Belgians.'

'For Christ sake, what about him?'

'Those known as decent folk reviled him and would consider sex between us as taboo, an old man's attempt to find satisfaction in the corruption of extreme youth and purity.'

'"They"! When did "their" morality become ours?'

'I can't help imagining the weight of public disgust falling over me, and it leaves a whiff; you look to see if you've trodden in something nasty.'

'Leave them to their filth, and let's get on with making another kind of world for ourselves.'

Liz was murmuring names in her sleep, those of girls in her class, you said, who'd been her tormentors. You made a sign to me to keep quiet. No, yours wasn't among them.

You leant over the aquarium (to see the time? To enter momentarily the green shadows that was for you a tangible reflection of what you'd just called our world?)

'What do you see when you look in there?'

A smile I had come to know as your happier one, smiled when I asked, or answered, one of our 'secret' questions.

'Up here the lords of the earth are the ones with the cruellest weapons, but down there the shy and timid come out of hiding and open their mouths for the crumbs.'

'Without an occasional strategic retreat into the small fragment of the legendary, original garden, human life becomes impossible.'

'Who said that?'

'Fintan F. Sugrue, in his unpublished, perhaps unpublishable, piece of true fiction: "The Desert City".'

'Anything else?'

'In the world to-day, gentlemen, without a certain margin of tranquillity man succumbs. But that's not Sugrue.'

'I succumbed too when I'd no refuge, nothing, at my first boarding school.'

'The convent?'

'The one before that. Some of the older girls despised me when I was crying at night because the gardener was going to do away with the puppies that his mongrel bitch had just had. One night soon after, when I pulled back the sheet there was one of the drowned puppies in my bed.'

What I'd taken for a nightdress struck me now, when I had a more detached look at it, as a summer dress. But for all I knew the night attire of the young was as bizarre as some of their street garments.

'It's a regular kitchen garden,' I said with a hand on a large rhubarb-like leaf imprinted on the cloth, 'with the foliage so thick there's no getting at the fruit and vegetables.'

'What about the slugs?'
'What about them?'
'They creep underneath.'
The finger-slug: a small and familiar creature. Penis: semi-savage, habits unknown, as yet, by you.
What had seemed my last-minute evasion a little earlier had made you wonder whether, besides being born 'with a different face', your body wasn't a properly-working sex machine. All the same, hadn't there been some relief, otherwise why keep on your knickers?
The thinly-veiled invitation to the lesser, more-domesticated of the two above-categorised maurauders couldn't be ignored without these new fears of yours, and Christ knows you'd enough already, being confirmed.
Melt and moan, moan and melt them away, at least partly reassured about your womanhood (though I foresaw the objection that occurred to you later), hiding your face and stifling a cry that would have woken the dead, let alone Liz, by pressing your mouth to the pillow.

TEN

No, you didn't long remain satisfied with what you called three-quarter measures that couldn't show you the sign you needed of my response. You both longed and dreaded to feel the breath of the fiery dragon come to claim you.

'Try and imagine I'm the girl hiker.'

'That would be as near blasphemy as I've ever been.'

I've skipped a day or two which I'll go back over in a minute, if only on Liz's account; I wanted to finish with what I see as the first phase of our relationship.

'She must have been a very attractive girl to make you want her in spite of the funeral.'

'What do you know about shameful urges? You'll never arouse them, not even now when you're legally and morally taboo. Didn't I tell you what you are?'

You shook your head, anxious, expectant.

'Didn't I, when I was showing the Old Testament pictures? You're a Rachel whose purpose wasn't the usual child-bearing but the casting of a pure, gentle light into the brutal darkness around her, though it was no more brutal than ours now. It worried her that she was different from her sister and their serving girls. After Leah had borne Jacob several children in quick succession she begged him: "Give me a child or I die".'

Never had I had such an audience as you.

'She was the first in the long succession of women that led through the Marys in the Gospel, through Beatrice, whom Dante fell in love with when she was thirteen, to Shakespeare's Miranda who came before the swallows dared and braved the winds of March.'

'But Rachel did have children.'

'Only after a mysterious delay of several years. She wasn't robust by Old Testament standards but she wasn't barren either, and I like to think that her non-fertility was the earliest recorded sign that lovemaking has another purpose. Later she had two children, dying when she gave birth to the second.'

I knew how raptly you'd listen to the repetition of these old tales, but now you must bear with some of the lesser mythologies in this record, those which involve your governess.

Liz woke to her first morning in the loft with another raging thirst, in fact had never really recovered from the earlier one to which was now added the further dehydration from all the wine we'd plied her with to ease her over the transition to the hiding-place.

This was something that not only had you foreseen but made quite unexpected provision for. On such mornings at school, you explained, she would go between classes to a café that catered principally for the schoolgirls and family parties of tourists and there ordered long, pastel-hued drinks in whose cloudy, icy depths floated slices of exotic fruits and, perhaps, portions of ice-cream. You and a couple of fellow spies had noted from your corner observation post the bliss with which she had imbibed these.

I now realised the providence that had made you lay

in the bottled syrups, tinned fruit and drinking straws, hygienically wrapped in pairs, that had somewhat surprised me at the time of unpacking.

I watched you with admiration taking the concomitants from the fridge and mixing your witch's brew. Then, still in your leafy night-attire over which you tied on a small, frilly apron (a delightful touch that, all the same, I was afraid might be indulging your love of 'let's-pretend' to the point where your governess might take offence) you served it on a tray.

Liz, meanwhile up and dressed, was slumped on a chair at the table, evidently unable to face the kitchenette to help prepare breakfast. She looked up expecting the inevitable toast, probably hoping for tea rather than coffee and saw a vision that made her raise her heavy eyelids and exclaim: 'Why, Herra!' Or rather, lapsing into the language of the school, or perhaps café: '*Aber*, *Herra*,' stressing the first syllable of your name (my tendency was to linger over the second).

How long could you keep her in your make-believe, lakeside café sucking the iced drink through a straw?

But right away there was one of those hitches that accompany states of nervous non-coordination to which extreme hangovers belong. An ovaloid of icecream half afloat at the top of the glass must have struck her as an obstacle to the free imbibing of the Sundae (as you'd called the concoction), as it could have been if she was intending to take some deep gulps from the glass before using the straws. With one of these she prods the creamy mass which sinks deeper (why the change of tense, I hear you object) causing, as a normally alert mind would have foreseen, the liquid to overflow.

Liz raised her till-now preoccupied glance, gingerly so

as not to increase the incipient dizziness by a sudden shift of scene, and looked imploringly round. For the waitress to come and mop up the mess? But you made no move.

In a game like this played on the nerves by subtle touches (a strange counterpart of the sensual one you'd got involved in earlier) you were at home and excelled. It reminded me of the art of the novelist, and I understood that having set the first scene in the café with everything deftly under control, neither you nor the imaginative writer would refuse situation or character the freedom to evolve in a manner not envisaged in the original plan.

You were sitting on the edge of your unmade bed, meditatively combing your hair with an idle finger, one side behind an ear while the thick strands on the other side of the parting fell forward, then the process in reverse.

The situation was too uncertain and precarious, as so often in a fiction too, to try to control according to plan. Let it go, let chance take a hand, and who's to say, not I, that it will lead to the deadlock or deadend that's the bane of both life and art.

What was she looking for? The paper napkin perhaps that had ever been to hand in happier (as, in spite of all, they now seemed to her?) times, an amenity that, at a guess, didn't exist within twenty miles.

The viscous cloud was spreading over the table-top towards the edge. Either the movement of her legs from under the table required an adroitness and resolution that she couldn't muster in time, or a full grasp of the logical course of events was beyond her. She sat still, more than still, as if trapped, swallowed (not a cooling drop had as yet touched her tongue) and the pastel-coloured liquid began a drip, drip onto the Sunday dress she was still wearing.

I filled a bowl with hot water in the kitchen, added a squeeze of washing-up liquid, snatched up a dish cloth, and was kneeling beside the shocked Liz inside the minute (as they time it in the all-action chronicles).

Soak rag in mixture of water and chemical cleanser, wonderfully mild, if the ads don't lie, lightly wring out and apply to the semi-obscene pale blobs on the black cloth. A gentle pressure, a quick squeeze out over the bowl and a circular wiping from the centre outward, aware of Liz's thigh a little above the knee and of her head bowed, like mine, over her lap, as if (*your* thought) she was holding the Infant Jesus and I was one of the Three Wise Men.

Hadn't there been a sudden closing-in between us when you'd fed the leveret from the glass dropper? There was a similar if lesser moment of communication between me and your governess that all my talking hadn't achieved. She murmured something, hardly opening her mouth, because, I guessed, she was afraid it was so close to mine I'd catch her fumey breath. The tone gave the gist of what she was expressing: her small, heart-felt, half-trust in another person, a feeling she hadn't imagined, let alone indulged in, for a long time.

'When it dries there'll be nothing left, not the smallest trace.'

I cleaned the table surface, not forgetting the bottom of the glass in which I placed the one still-serviceable straw, and stiffly got to my feet. You and I breakfasted together in the tiny kitchen. I had an idea that we should have stayed with Liz but, when it came to it, I was too curious to see how you'd behave in the cool light of morning when we were alone together. If I had expected signs of embarrassment I was shown my mistake.

Between mouthfuls of coffee you stretched the dual-purpose day or night attire you were wearing and revealed, over your belly, some torn stitches (had you used a scissors?) between two of the cotton leaves, 'to let the ancient slug crawl through when nobody (meaning Liz) is looking'.

I didn't have to follow precisely what you had in mind to realize that I'd a lot to learn about the generation to which you didn't quite belong. The dark, secret, semi-shameful sexuality of my youth for you didn't exist. You saw it partly as a game of skill you wanted to shine at, as a respite from the fears that beset you at most other times, as an easy and pleasant alternative to all the things that either bored or frightened you, but not as sacred to two people, not as a marriage bond which was the old shutting out and shutting in in another form.

You, who were born so serious, didn't take sex very seriously once you'd got over your initial doubts about your own sex appeal.

It was Mullen's suggestion rather than our love-making that was on your mind. You thought I was going to refuse, as I might have hadn't our position been so precarious.

'I think you should accept.'

'Do we want to get mixed up with that crowd?'

'I don't want to get mixed up with any crowd, but if we have to they don't sound bad.'

'You liked Mullen?'

'He didn't much like *me*. We couldn't be frank with him about our relationship.'

'Not with any of his lot.'

Though come to that, with what 'lot' (apart from my poet friends) could we?

'Living in a station sounds fun.'

Well, yes, perhaps; but at my age that wasn't the term I'd have used. Besides, here and now there was enough 'fun' to keep me going.

When Liz, having finished two of the exotic concoctions you'd prepared for her, came back from the bathroom (where I suspect she had surreptitiously swallowed a couple of glasses of plain water) ship-shape, except for the puffiness under the eyes, and in her weekday dress with white collar and cuffs, she announced the start of lessons at the big table.

'Just a minute, Mrs. Considine,' I heard you say before you were standing close to me in the kitchenette, your red-rimmed eyes (lack of sleep or emotion or both left tell-tale traces on you) wide with apprehension.

'Let's open a bottle of wine with her and get her back where she was yesterday. Come on, quick, sweet Jesus, before she calls me.'

'Calm down, Herra. It wouldn't work, not so early and without being led up to.'

Anyhow I didn't think a panicky improvisation would help in planning the next few days, whereas your hopes were more modest.

'I couldn't bear it, not now. Maths!'

'Darling, please go through with it. It gives us a breathing space and later I'll have a talk with your governess. Besides, its a mental exercise not altogether useless for life on this globe.'

You had taken up some dishes that I'd already dried and were wiping them with deliberate slowness.

'For me this globe, as you call it, and all its exercises, educational, religious and sporting, have long ago been written off.'

'Amen. For God's sake leave those cups, I've done them.'

You left them back on the table obediently, bowed your head and murmured: 'Come and rescue me soon.'

What a morning it looked like being! After a far from uneventful night. A morning whose dawning we had celebrated with (if your conventual schedule was correct) the appropriate psalms, followed by the fantasy of the strange tale of the field mouse, or snail, or other unnamable creature, under the leaves in the water-vegetable jungle-garden.

Which brought me back with a shock to the rent in the lower front of your ambiguous garment, all the more obsessional for being unnoticeable and that would be doubly hidden as you sat at the table with your governess, chin on palms, hair a motionless wet-withered-leaf-coloured cascade.

To try to enter a more equitable frame of mind I withdrew to my 'study', as I hoped to transform what otherwise was a bleak little waiting-room into. I plunged into one of the afore-mentioned books, a volume on Ecology, whose first law, as I had just learnt, is that in Nature everything is connected with everything else. Which brought me right back to you, for I took it as an explanatory comment on the reopening of the wounds on your wrists. The other books had much the same message in less scientific terms; I reread the passage in Dostoevski where Father Zosima speaks of communing with birds, and a poem of John Clare's, who spent a time in Northampton asylum, about his hares.

'Come and rescue me at the first opportunity!' You needn't have feared I'd delay. I'd supposed I knew what it was to be old: the blunting of the sharp, minor physical pains that youth is susceptible to such as toothache, a stone in the shoe, neuralgia, backache. And a corresponding relaxation of the feverish, impatient longings. But, though you were there on the other side of the thin partition, quite safe and without the possibility of escaping, the half-hours and quarter-hours until I was due to come and stand with a tray of coffee things beside the table where you were sitting dragged interminably.

You were drawing me with your let's-pretend half-aroused body, with your Rachel-Magdalen-Miranda-Ophelia psyche.

For all the expanse of Ecosphere in which I was immersed I was never freed from the brooding consciousness of the rent in your dress nor, on the other level, of the way in which you could give the image of a small tormented creature a greater intensity of horror and panic than the great painters had evoked with their crucifixions.

ELEVEN

I, who was patient and inured to waiting, not just for part of a morning but for years, had the tray ready and the water boiling, the electricity switched off again, three minutes, and once more on, a hopeful glance at the kitchen clock, and off. Where was the tranquil solitude of long winter evenings, nobody coming, then, or for all I knew, ever, no car stopping, no crunch of shoe on the gravel, the telephone as dumb as the blue jug on the shelf above it?

Communing with the dead, Lodwick, my animals, even Nancy, they initiated me into their patience, having learnt to wait timelessly and for whom now, as I resurrected them, the most uneventful days and nights could never be too long.

In the end I entered the big room five minutes too soon and Liz looked first at the tray and then at her watch but, surprising me with your unexpected diligence, you didn't raise your head from an open book. When I got near I saw that over the page of what looked like equations there was a photo you'd torn from a newspaper. Evidently taken surreptitiously from a distance with a telescopic lens, it showed a number of hares herded together against a wire fence. The caption: 'Waiting for Death.' And in the rather indistinct picture they, by something in their postures, seemed to be waiting with the patience of non-human nature.

You closed the book without looking up, waiting, I guessed, before raising your face from its shelter of hair till it had lost some of the look of horror that, unlike most of us, familiarity with its cause never lessened for you.

You spoke afterwards of the minutely mottled hares' coats, that you'd remarked in the leveret, that with their hi-fi ears and fleetness was their principal defence. This singular sign of natural shyness and vulnerability (yours was your veiling hair) they were shamefully stripped of in the prison where it was purposeless.

Liz, not catching the glimpse of the tall, slender bottle that had been her form of obsession most of the morning, was (this too I believed I was registering on my novelist's interception device) disappointed.

'Herra refuses to concentrate on her lessons,' she said, 'and we'll have to return to the downstairs room where there are fewer distractions.'

How much did she know or suspect of the real story of your defection from the group of which she'd been second-in-charge? The papers had been reticent; it wasn't the straightforward kind of scandal they can safely exploit.

'I've got to lie low for a bit; you don't know what's been happening in this land of ours in recent times.'

'Surely at your age you're not involved; I mean in any illegal goings on.'

'His age has nothing to do with it,' you exclaimed.

Not the wisest intervention, and it drew your governess's attention to something she apparently hadn't noticed: your air of exhaustion, evident around the eyes and in your lack-lustre hair. She was seeing you for the first time since our night out.

'Please leave Mr. Sugrue and me alone for a few minutes.'

'Do *you* want me to?'

Your appealing to me was making it worse.

'Do what Liz asks you.'

What an air of loss, of absence, descended on the table the moment you were gone to the other side of the partition! The abandoned cup of coffee, the school book with the photo shut between its pages, the deserted water-garden, they signalled to me intimations of loss.

'It's my duty to ask you a painful question,' Liz was saying. Hadn't she got it wrong, shouldn't it be: 'It's my painful duty . . .? (At tense moments the thoughts scatter like birds at a shot.)

'Have you assaulted her?'

'The assaults that Herra endures aren't the kind that most people find shocking.'

'Perhaps not. But I'm putting the question in the crude, simple sense. And if you have, I don't say I'd be particularly shocked, she'd have provoked it, but it would mean the end of our staying here.'

No air of moral outrage, though it's true I hadn't made a formal plea of 'guilty'. I think that since I'd knelt and cleaned up her dress she realised something she couldn't as yet formulate: such as that we both belonged among the less-than-respectable and that to have found even a distant sharer in her secret made it, if not less shameful, less lonely.

This was the moment, with Liz's question, like most urgent questions, not so much answered as put in doubt as to being the right one, that you flew silently across the expanse of loft and were beside me, bending down and saying: 'They're here!'

You'd spent your banishment standing on the kitchen table looking from the skylight that faced towards garden and drive. You paused, your hair falling over both our faces, giving us a brief refuge before the hounds had sniffed us out, and whispered low enough for Liz not to catch: 'Two priests.'

A mid-morning call by the parish priest accompanied by a colleague who happened to be on holiday from, say, Nottingham? An unmotivated above-board, pastoral visitation, made in innocent good faith?

'The bloody spies!'

This time you spoke loud enough for Liz to hear. If she'd been wondering what piece of private information had brought you so precipitously back to communicate to me (among her more fanciful explanations: you'd had an intimation of the return of your period, thus relieving our shared misgivings?), this didn't enlighten her.

'Who is it?'

No, not so much spies for the law as guardians of the moral rural climate, though should they catch something other than the homely, pious, unhygienic smells, connoting for them purity, they might bay loud enough to cause the local guards to investigate.

'Father Daly and a friend of his.'

'Aren't you going to let them in?'

'No.'

This plain negative seemed to upset Liz more than my not-quite straightforward answer to her other query.

'I think we should.'

She had only to call down the trap-door to them to put an end to a situation that she'd been about to tell me couldn't go on.

Another knock, prolonged, peremptory.

You were back at your lookout post and I was beside you waiting to hear the next move in the assault. (Assault! I was back at Liz's question. Which terrified you the more, this, or my hesitant, half-attempt before I'd realised the presence of the cotton curtain as we'd lain on your bed?)

I'd left Liz alone, free to act as conscience, instinct, self-preservation or whatever guide she followed at moments of crisis impelled her.

'They're peeping in the window.'

I had purposely left the curtains undrawn.

My face was close to the invisible cleavage in your dress: had anyone asked me (at last the relevant question!) on what few centimetres of centrality the cosmos was at this moment balanced I could have answered unambiguously, nothing could have stopped me answering, with a tip of a finger, or, better, my tongue (as the more precise and sensitive indicator) on the hidden entrance.

You were trembling.

The psalm that I'd also been re-reading while impatiently awaiting the morning break came back to me: 'My heart hath become as wax.'

There came back too the newspaper photo, the creatures still unaware of what was in store, ears not yet flat, one even with front paws up on each side of its face, washing. Nature still throbbed with its universal faint beat in them, but at the first barking the fragile apparatus that links us all, and you and them more particularly, would, in the words of the psalmist, melt.

'I can't see them now; they must be at the door of the garage.'

So far no sound from the main part of the loft, such as one side of the trap-door being lifted.

'They're back at the bedroom window.'
'Making sure the bed's empty.'
'They're standing there talking.'
'You've seen enough.'

I put my arms round your middle and, with you folding over my shoulder, and my mouth against the cotton foliage (imagining I felt the cloth parting), lifted you off the table.

Lifting you down was as precarious and exciting a manoeuvre as that performed by the ice skater who, after raising his partner high with hands on the inside of her wide-apart thighs, shifts his grip to her waist and lowers her with inspired skill at precisely the right angle onto the edge of her skates. That's how it felt: a breathtaking act, and, after placing you safely on the floor, I kept a hold on you to steady you in the imaginary pas-de-deux (though, for all I know the figure in question is called a 'lutz').

You clung to me as if you were finding difficulty in regaining your balance. When I bent my head to kiss your cheek, your face slid slightly out of position as by chance in the shift of relative positions as we circled the arena, and our mouths met.

'Don't you wish I was eighteen, or twenty-eight?' you withdrew yours to ask.

'I do not. What matters is that in your short stay on this earth you've grasped as much, or more, about the true situation as I during my prolonged one.'

Liz was calling. Returning to the main loft, leaving you, at your suggestion, to wash up the coffee cups (a way of not having immediately to meet your governess's glance), I saw she hadn't moved from the table.

'What did they want?'

Did she think I'd talked to them from the kitchen skylight? I shook my head.

'Perhaps Mrs. Friedlander asked the parish priest to keep an eye on Herra.'

'I shouldn't wonder.'

'You encourage the child in her neurotic world of make-believe.'

'Suppose Pilate had asked: "What is make-believe?" he might have received the answer: "*I* am make-believe."'

TWELVE

Not that I actually offered Liz this speculation; instead, I pleaded with her to let you off lessons for the rest of the morning. We both realised that the 'serious talk' between us that had been started and then left in the air was imminent.

'I shall write to her.'

For me at the moment all 'hers' not more precisely defined referred to you and I imagined her scribbling a note to be delivered by me to the kitchen.

'To Mrs. Friedlander?'

'Telling her I think her daughter should return home.'

'Do you still not grasp, Liz, how fatal it would be to try to force her?'

'Fatal? Aren't you exaggerating?'

'She's a constant spectator of scenes of agony and violent death (and don't say: "only in her make-believe world" because that doesn't signify) that the rest of us only catch distant glimpses, and hear echoes, of. That's why she clings so little to life.'

'Dr. Heilbrunn diagnosed severe neurosis.'

'Just a minute; let's leave this new and somewhat sinister-sounding expert out while I finish. If her mother tries to take her home the fragile weight that keeps her inner scales precariously tilting on the side of life will be jolted back on the other one.'

'The net of the hunters': another of the phrases from the psalms we'd recited; it wasn't that I persuaded Liz that if you thought it was closing tighter round you you'd take the only way you saw of escape, but, as most arguments are decided, she arrived at a conclusion that she'd been trying to evade, with perhaps some slight help from me.

Though for totally different reasons, we agreed that we couldn't stay much longer where we were. I suggested a move to the city. We'd stay at a hotel and she could telephone your mother and, with her approval, make further plans. It wasn't yet the moment to mention the ghetto in the northern town.

'If you feel I'm hiding from you're not sure what authorities for reasons you can only guess at, you'll feel better with a more social existence.'

This was as far as I went then towards preparing her for the Laggan. I'd had to promise that we'd leave the next day and stay in a city hotel while considering our next move which would be influenced by the outcome of the telephone call to your mother she was going to make.

Just as it was time for lunch and you were laying the table, you stopped halfway to the kitchen, standing stock-still in the centre of the big, bare room like a creature that comes to a sudden halt in its tracks, and swivels its ears.

'Christ! What's that?'

You flew to your lookout at the skylight.

Horses' hooves on the road and accents, penetrating enough to reach our threatened haven, evoking utter self-assurance and pitched on a thrilled note at the prospect of being about to have sluggish nerves titivated.

'Where on earth are they going?'

Hunting you hadn't yet been confronted with. Unlike coursing, there was little or nothing about it for you to read in the papers, and you came from a foreign city where you wouldn't have heard of it.

What to tell you? Not less than the facts, however much I wanted to shield you. Far from living in what for Liz, or your mother, was a make-believe world, you had to endure the realities of the factual one.

'They're looking for something, probably a fox, to chase to death.'

Ask no more for to-day, my love.

You sat on the table, not looking at me in your dejection.

'You promised her we'd leave here to-morrow.'

Another 'her', one of 'them', the enemy. You'd been listening behind the partition, incidentally.

'It's not safe here any longer.'

'Is it safe in the city?'

'Not for us together. But I don't intend we stay there.'

A pause; one of those when I tried to say something comforting and didn't know what.

'Then this might be our last time together.'

A bright evasion was worse than silence.

'For Christ's sake don't abandon me.'

'Let's leave Christ out of it.'

'Did He reprimand Mary Magdalen for spending the night after the crucifixion with her lover?'

'What on earth makes you think that?'

'Instinct.'

'You should try not to improve on the Gospels.'

'You can't leave me alone with the sounds of the hunt all night.'

'They don't hunt at night.'

A statement true only of one world, and that one not yours.

'You'd protect what crept into your bed or your arms for shelter, hare or fox?'

You'd changed into jeans, Liz having told you you must make up your mind whether you wore the leaf pattern garment at night or during the day, for she couldn't allow you to keep it on continuously. And you'd put on a sweater whose sleeves covered your wrists.

'If you join it to yours, my body won't be exposed to them.'

Had you simply offered yourself as occasionally other girls, though older ones, had, I'd have been free not to have to take it very seriously. But you were affording an excuse for me to succumb to the most intense of any desire that had ever obsessed me.

There was still Liz. There were three bottles of wine left of our original store, sufficient possibly to both share with her halfway to oblivion and leave enough for her to complete the journey on. But I didn't think this was a trick that could be repeated a second or third time.

You agreed to appear punctually at the table in the main loft for the afternoon session with Liz and I made you the promise. Promise? Rather an admission that I'd no choice but to abet you in your all-or-nothing resolve.

You waited anxiously for dusk to fall and the hunt be called off, one preoccupation, among others, that prevented you pleasing your governess that afternoon any better than you had in the morning.

Six. The hour when for how many autumns and springs I came in from my last stroll around the plot as dusk fell and stood at the cooker in a trance of memories for the few moments that it took for the electric rings to glow and it was time to start preparing the evening meal. Now it was perhaps the last of all the hours of six that I should ever celebrate in this place by taking bearings on the time of year, the weather, the quality of the light and the angle of certain shadows.

'What are you doing? Where are you going?'

Who had broken into my private farewells?

'Down to make a couple of phone calls.'

'I'll come with you,' it was Liz, 'and book a call to Mrs. Friedlander.'

This you didn't overhear, having gone to the kitchen to chop vegetables for the soup, or salad, while, with the skylight open, you listened for the return of the hunt, not knowing that by now it was far away and wouldn't be coming back by the route it had set out.

I let Liz book her call before dialling mine. First the home from home for the cats (the fish could accompany us to a hotel) which, though I knew you wouldn't think much of, would be tolerable for a brief stay. Then Mullen, to make an appointment and give him a message for Peter about the car which I'd have to sell to raise the money for the move, being at the end of what your mother had given me. In any case a car with character, whose registration number had been noted by the guardians of the law, was no longer going to be safe transport.

When I returned to the loft, leaving Liz to await her call, you were peering down through the trap door with too-staring eyes.

'Where, in God's name, have you been?'

I told you, and also where your governess was, and you put your arms round me and hugged me to you as if I'd returned from a long journey.

I was at the table to make a note of the name of the pub where I was to meet Mullen, with my back to the trap door, when there was a crash from the garage. As I turned you were closing it, having managed (where had the strength come from?) to dislodge the ladder.

'Later, we'll throw her down her bedclothes.'

I'd been conscious, as the threats to it increased, of our world, as happens I suppose in all citadels as the siege intensifies, becoming more and more a place where the outside norms were invalid. Precarious fantasy was now our reality; I'd seen it coming and done nothing to prevent it.

The noise had brought Liz to the garage. You, like a naughty child scared at what it's done, had disappeared.

'What is it? What's happened?'

Keep it coolly factual, with plenty of detail.

'The end of the steps got caught in the trap door and slipped from where it was anchored to the crossbeam.'

She made an attempt and failed to lift the narrower end of the ladder from the garage floor.

'What on earth are we going to do now?'

'Luckily, I've just sent Peter word to come with the car in the morning. If he parks it directly underneath I can lower myself to its roof and the two of us will get the steps in position again.'

'And what about me?'

'No problem, Liz. We'll roll up your bedclothes with your supper and a bottle of wine in the bundle and lower them to the castaway.'

The telephone rang from the cottage, giving me a respite as breaker-of-bad news. I found you in the bathroom, the last of the three tiny compartments beyond the partition.

'What's the matter?'

'Don't *you* start asking.'

You withdrew the fingers you'd been stopping your ears with so as not to overhear my conversation with Liz in case you found you had now two stern judges; three, if your governess had got through to your mother.

'Let's get her things to her so that we can pull up our drawbridge.'

'How can you pull it up?'

You weren't registering. I had first to calm you down and by now words alone wouldn't do; the full flow of tenderness could only reach you through the raw nerves and senses.

A long embrace from which, at last, I gently disentangled you.

'I'd like to get the trap shut again soon. That's what I meant.'

'Ah.'

Had you not taken it in? It didn't matter, your distraction was no longer painful.

You helped make up the bundle that, when securely fastened with cord, resembled part of a Red Cross consignment to be dropped from the air to flood or famine victims. But when I brought it to the trap in readiness for lowering you disappeared.

When Liz arrived in the garage, and before I could get the survival kit down to her, she told me the news, that she didn't hide had come as a great relief to her: your mother was flying over and would meet us in the city the next day.

'Mrs. Friedlander was worried to death because we hadn't phoned as you or Herra had, she said, promised. The crazy child hasn't even written.'

There *had* been mention of keeping in close touch and your mother had put through several calls without reply, but even Liz had lost all sense of time and was putting the blame on us.

'Where on earth is she?'

Why the 'on earth.' Though in a moment the phrase was given unexpected relevance.

The bundle made a perfect landing at the cast-away's feet.

'I had to make an excuse about her not coming to the phone.'

'The longer we stay here talking, Liz, the more chance of our being overheard by snooping neighbours.'

'I'd feel happier if . . .'

You appeared (that's the only way of putting it), an apparition framed in the opening in the floor of the loft. You stood in your cotton night attire that you'd changed back into, hands crossed on breast, looking down with what was such a good imitation of a heavenly smile that the next cue in the little comedy—whether black or white I wasn't sure—was for Liz to drop to her knees. Which of course your governess had neither the heart nor imagination for. You disappeared from her view with what was part pirouette, part ethereal withdrawal from human eyes.

'She's out of her senses!'

'Liz, let's say good-night.'

'You encourage her.'

'Don't turn on the light and if anyone knocks don't open the door.'

THIRTEEN

'I've dreamed of hearing that sound for as long as I remember, listening to it getting nearer.'

'What sound?'

'The noise the hounds make, and, when I wake, my heart, like in the psalms, has turned to wax.'

You were slumped at the table that you were supposed to be laying with a touch of festivity for our last evening meal here. In front of you were the newspaper cuttings and a paperback about our island fauna that you said had been one of your first purchases on that day of extended shopping, and that I hadn't seen before.

'I'll read you a bit from the report of The Greyhound Coursing Club about why hares are almost extinct in parts of the country.'

Had it been to go once more into this obsessional subject with me without interruption that you had taken the drastic means to prevent the return of your governess? The question was another of those that are useless to ask and cannot be accurately answered. I'd put it to myself in momentary irritation.

'"Numbers of hares", you were reading, "are run down by motorists at night, often deliberately." Why do they make this out to be more cruel than setting hounds on them?'

'For one thing its not in the interests of commercialised sport. And I suppose they argue there's no close season for the car hunts.'

'Swift, but not fast enough to escape and find the hidden exit from the blinding path of cruel light, that's something I know well. The agonising instinct of self-preservation and the even deeper, more unconscious one that I only grasp now when you mention the close season. The secret rendezvous that will never be kept.'

'Rendezvous?'

'With what are waiting hidden under leaves and fur from the mother's breast in a thicket.'

'I see.'

'How could I dream all this before I'd read these?'

'Because, I think, you're a more integral part of nature's closed circle than most of us.'

'Those in the car had probably forgotten their thrill by the end of their drive, but for me it's one of the dreams I'll never get over.'

'Come, Herra, it's time to eat.'

'I'll be going home with my mother after all.'

But hadn't I entered far enough into your secret mind, or let's say some areas of it, not to be too surprised at what went on there? No good starting to argue when you were where argument couldn't reach you, having retreated, or been driven, to one of its dark recesses. First try to bring you back towards where you didn't feel so frightened and alone.

'Now that you've managed our being alone, let's begin sharing our last evening here.'

'How?'

'With supper, first of all.'

'I mean what I say.'

'You always mean what you say, at least to me. What you meant just now to convey to Liz is another matter.'

'To tell her that, from tomorrow, I'd be a little angel.'

You were brushing first one side of your hair and then the other behind an ear with your finger; perhaps because it needed a slight sideways tilt of the head to keep the just-arranged one in place, both sides were never caught back together.

It wasn't very difficult to persuade you to help me prepare the meal and by the time it came to the little ceremony of opening our very last bottle of wine your heart was in it. Oh yes, it was always possible for someone, or some creature (like Lazarella) who had the key to it, to open your heart.

At first there was a hush over the supper table, like that, you remarked, on Christmas morning at breakfast before you were let open your presents, or even see them, so that you weren't even sure (something I easily understood of you) that there'd be any.

The breaking of the age-old ecological cycle was setting up stresses that nature had never till now had to endure and this was having repercussions on those psyches most closely linked in the circle. (I was trying to explain to myself your dream.)

Voices outside the door of the garage.

'Gentle Jesus!'

'It's only the kids from opposite; they think we've left.'

You were round the table and in my arms.

'Liz has told them we're here.'

'Oh, no. They wouldn't show themselves openly then; they'd whisper and peep through the hedges.'

You had your fingers in your ears.

All the sounds from outside were threatening! the priests' car at the gate, the hunt passing, the ring of the phone to tell Liz her call was through (that you'd listened for without hearing), Liz herself underneath.

'Shall I put on a record?'

'They'd hear it.'

'Not if I turn the sound low.'

You shook your head violently.

'Hide me!'

'How?'

'You know how, but you can't.'

'Can't!'

'Then hide me, hide me from all this!'

It couldn't go quite so smoothly and quickly as you, in your panic, wanted it to. You were in such a hurry to be assured that it worked. But I heard you murmur to yourself: '*Das tut mir Weh.*'

When, after a moment, I asked were you all right, you said: '*Ça va*', slipping into what you must have thought, in the stress of the moment, was my language.

To my last, on-the-point-of-no-return question: 'You won't regret it?' your reply rang out like the responses you'd made in reciting the psalms: '*Non, je ne regrette rien!*'

Nor was I myself, not even that half-self that previously I'd managed to preserve during love-making. Now I didn't know where I was, the end walls of the loft seemed to be gone and I had a glimpse far beyond them of distant figures, one of whom might have been your mother and another Nancy, but they were too indistinct to recognise. Could they see *us*?

What was that, what were you murmuring? 'When the sparks fly out of the log let them go up the chimney.'

Having safely negotiated what you'd seen as pitfalls, the one you'd feared most being your undesirability, you were ready to brave all lesser risks. As you put it afterwards, we ended up doing, what for days we'd been tinkering at, truly and properly.

The public, active part of the next day started earlier than I'd anticipated with Peter arriving in the Rolls just as we'd got the cats into their travelling basket and the fish in a bowl covered with perforated plastic.

The car was backed in so that the roof was under the opening to the loft and a sack thrown over its shiny surface for me to drop onto after hanging by my hands from the ledge round the trap door. We replaced the car by the ladder and I went up again to conduct the evacuation. Liz stood waiting for you to appear, what she expected to read in your face or general bearing wasn't difficult to guess from her expression of mingled anxiety and curiosity.

I took a last look round the plot. As I stopped at the first of the memorial slabs, trying to imagine I had paused in my usual morning stroll, that I was looking at it from the midst of my former isolation and silence, you were suddenly beside me.

'This isn't goodbye to your treasures; as I told you I've decided to go home with my mother.'

FOURTEEN

But, of course, it wasn't difficult to persuade you that my 'treasures' were, no, not in any sense diminished, but no longer where they had been all these years. They had become part of the world I shared with you and wherever we went they would accompany us. There was no need for you to leave me with them by giving yourself up to your mother and face another of the institutions in which you had come so near to despair.

Now for your last words in the loft, that is one of the passages that the main purpose of this report is to record and preserve: 'Last night was the first for ages I slept without one of those dreams and woke without the soreness in chest and wrists.'

Note for my own enlightenment: prolonged exposure to mental and emotional shock causes nerve inflammation that can seem to be located in certain areas; in the main sensory but non-erogenous zones.

At the hotel you were worried that I'd book a double room for you and your governess, and never left my side while I was at the reception desk. Although Liz couldn't have drunk more than the bottle of wine I had lowered to her in the bundle, she was almost as withdrawn as in one of her hangovers. This you explained by the coming meeting with your mother, the prospect of which frightened her.

'What about you?'

'I'm not frightened of her any more.'

'Since when?'

I guessed the answer but wanted to hear it from you.

'Since last night.'

I realised that by becoming lovers a new relationship is formed, even if in many, or most, cases it is immediately annulled by an unconscious act of will, and that, whether or not the couple have official recognition as close relatives, they are stamped, however accidentally or incongruously, with the consanguinous seal. What I'm getting at in my tortuous fashion is what you grasped instinctively that if you 'belonged' to anyone it was to me rather than to your mother.

'Three single rooms, two with bath.' This extravagance was to facilitate the smuggling in of the cats which we hoped to accommodate in the bathroom belonging to yours, and that would also be needed when it came to transferring the fish back to the large tank. And I couldn't seem to relegate your governess to what she might see as an inferior by not taking a similar luxury for her.

I lay on the bed in my room and caught a glimpse of myself in the mirror of public opinion that seemed to be part of the invisible furnishings of this place. Ah, Herra, where were the reassuring myths we'd shared in the loft? Who was this King-Leopold-of-the-Belgians figure wearing my mask?

I dare not go to your room, and what if you, too, suddenly, became aware of this 'reality' and shunned me?

You never knew till I tell you now how blessed to my ears was the scratching on my door that reminded me of the night at your mother's house when you'd come, with Lazarella, to tell me about the early-morning paper-round.

I had an appointment with Mullen in a backstreet pub and you begged me to take you with me.

'It might be safer we aren't seen together.'

'Who's bothering about us here?'

Was I not quite free of the doubts of a few moments ago? Or wasn't a look-out, if a negligent one, being kept for us?

'If anyone called about the car while I'm out you could let them have a look at it in the hotel car park.'

This was drawing you into the family circle of two, an extension on the practical level of the love-making of the night. And it didn't escape you; but, all the same: no. You'd renounce the excitement, when they rang my room from the desk, of saying, not quite that you were Mrs. S. but that you were acting for that gentleman during his temporary absence.

Our way led through a rather run-down street market and at its junction with a narrow alley we met a flock of sheep. A patter over the cobbles; an excruciatingly unrhythmic bobbing of the drooped heads as some were hobbling painfully on match-stick legs. One had sunk down and settled in the middle of the street with a deceptive air of quiet rest, doubled-under knees just protruding from beneath its fleece, that recalled the fields behind the cottage at sunset.

'Where are they going?'

I knew too well. To the dilapidated door in the crumbling wall of the lane with the just-distinguishable name above it in faded paint followed by the two words that left no doubt about the destination.

I might have told you: 'To be sheared,' but I couldn't.

You squatted down beside the exhausted beast, your face mercifully veiled by your hair from the curious glances of the passers-by, bowed in what struck me as shame beside the black, archaic-looking snout. A drover hurried over and prodded the sheep with his stick; it scrambled to its delicately pointed, ballerina's feet and trotted, with what seemed a patient submission that must have wrung your heart, after the others.

I led you back to the pavement and we continued along the busy streets to the pub.

Mullen was alone at a table in an alcove and at a larger, corner one I recognised with relief some old friends. I hadn't forgotten them, but the dead, like John Lodwick, are easier to evoke than the absent living, and I'd let long periods elapse without renewing my bond with them. Now I saw them as exposed and vulnerable as you, and to the same kind of harassment if in another form.

'This is Herra.' I told you the Christian names of the three poets: Bill, Hayden and John, and they took you to themselves as can only happen when innocents and victims meet and recognise each other almost without a word.

'The return of the hermit,' one of them commented with a smile.

'Not that anymore, it seems,' another remarked.

Part of you was absent, having followed the sheep to the end of their road, the other part seemed to feel itself safe in this company. I tried to get a look at your wrist as you sipped the beer they'd bought you but without my glasses, that I didn't want to put on and make you feel you were being scrutinised, the thin line was barely visible.

'I won't be long.'

'I'm all right.'

What better appreciation could the three poets have received than this coming spontaneously from one of the most anxious and wary of wild creatures?

You squeezed my hand, not hiding our relationship but not flaunting it either as you had to your governess.

'Wherever a few people are sufficiently hurt and shocked by the consumer society, or whatever name it gets from its dominant local character, they try to escape by any means they can, whether it's a few shacks in a park in an American city or some sheds in a French village, or, with us, a disused railway station.'

Mullen went straight to the point as soon as he'd ordered me a beer.

I asked him, as I think I had before in your presence but without getting a very clear answer, what had made them choose me to watch over the migration from one world to another and the change of heart, of all transformations the most revolutionary, involved.

'The Committee got hold of one of your books and passed it round, apparently they had only the one copy; don't ask me which, I'm not myself a great reader. But I did get through a piece you had in the paper a couple of months ago.'

All my life I'd been obsessed with my fictions, getting little in the way of response. And now when I'd come to see myself as the constructor of, and dweller in, a very private ghetto at the end of a derelict street in a part of town where only a few stray animals came, a group of militant young people, or perhaps that section of them who had rejected even militancy, wanted me to share it with them. To put it another way: I spent the earlier part of my life hopefully constructing a fiction, in instalments, against whose exposed length small charges were placed disguised as literary criticism and detonated from the distant safety of reviews. So finally I retired to an inner citadel, it's you I'm adressing now, not Mullen, who is contemplating his half-empty glass, his thoughts, on one of his rare trips south, concerned with other things than the proposal the Committee of Five had asked him to pass on to me, however hard this was for me to imagine. And then, in a state part tranquil, part disturbingly lonely, and in the silence of the obscurity into which, as a writer, I'd fallen out of ken of all but a few friends (some of them dead), the black shell on the strand where no wave ever washed had filled with whispers of the returning tide.

It was one of those times when your god of chance reveals himself. First the 'accident' of your school selecting this island as the place to which to send a group of its pupils, followed by Mullen's visit that, had it been a week earlier, would have prevented you finding me. And now the meeting with my three friends who seldom happened to be here together, and one of whom didn't even live in the city. Yes, I saw this encounter as also providential; they were there when I needed them most. Does this surprise you? Our conversation hadn't struck you as concerned with anything of particular importance.

No, I made nothing in the nature of a definite appeal to them, asked for no signed promise. Communication with poets whose poetry I can decode can be conducted as well by the silences between, as by the words themselves.

I didn't have to put my request dramatically, or even biblically. Nothing in the 'brothers, or, more appropriately, sons, behold your sister!' style. Some casual-seeming words were sufficient to indicate my anxiety to make minimum provision for you in a future when, in the normal course of time, I wouldn't be here to shelter you.

They gave their word without you being aware of it, and the word of a poet is, on the formally contractual level, less reliable, and on the other, vital one, more binding, than that of a more obviously responsible citizen. And we had another round of beer, with a glass of wine for you.

On the way back to the hotel I called into a small off-licence for a bottle of wine to bring back to Liz (she was on my mind) and as we waited to be served a dark, unshaved, wild-eyed apparition counted out in penny and twopenny pieces onto the counter the price of a bottle of locally-produced sherry. When the girl turned her back as she deposited the coins in the till a ragged sleeve was thrust across the counter, a hand emerged from it, grasped a second bottle and secreted it inside the front of the much-stained jacket.

Neither of us remarked on the incident; had we an inkling it might involve us more than we wished? I bought what I'd come for and we left the shop. Halfway down the alleyway the same sinister (as he was to me) figure was sitting on the cobbles with his back to the wall, one of the bottles of cheap sherry and another, smaller bottle with a chemist's label beside him.

He rose and sidled over to us, holding out his hand, not looking at us, the glitter in his eyes of bright, broken fragments. From his blackish mouth as he muttered his appeal came a whiff of the methylated spirits he mixed with the sherry.

I tried to pull you past him but you'd seen the faded sign above the gate. You pointed to it with a fifty penny piece.

'Let us have a look in there?'

He cupped his fingers with their blunt, broken-nailed tips, under the coin and, now looking at me but addressing you, asked: 'How long?'

'Just a few minutes, that's all.'

Did he nod? You let the coin drop and the death-dealing hand closed over it. With a large key he unlocked the wooden gates, enough for you to slip through and for me to follow you, stop, call you back and to feel the touch I winced away from pushing me in after you. I heard the gate relocked.

A walled and badly paved yard whose floor was wet with a trickle of pink water from under the door of the shed at its other end. In a corner a pile of rainbow-hued offal, steaming faintly.

'Look at their insides all mixed up together,' you said, 'and we think ours are mingled when we make love!'

'What's the point of that morbid remark?'

You opened your mouth, not to answer my irritated question, provoked by my own dismay, but, head bowed over and falling hair almost touching the wet concrete, to vomit. With an arm round your heaving middle, I found a handkerchief to wipe your lips.

'I couldn't pass by and not look; not even not look when it's all over.'

Ah, Herra, will you never spare yourself anything?

While keeping an arm around your heaving body, I knocked on the gate. No sign of our accomplice. Try again, make the old lock rattle!

'He's gone back to the shop with the money I gave him.'

'And forgotten us.'

'You know why he thought we wanted to be locked in here?'

'It crossed my mind.'

I kicked the gate in a semi-panic to get you out.

'For God's sake stop! Can't we bear it patiently with nothing happening to us for a short time?'

'That bloody butchering scum!'

'He's as much a victim as the creatures he kills.'

FIFTEEN

Back at the hotel you went to your room and I knocked on Liz's door.

'I've brought you a bottle of your favourite wine.'

A pleasantly reassuring remark recalling, as I meant it to, halcyon meetings and greetings between those without a care in the world.

'Mrs. Friedlander is here.'

'Ah.' Or Oh, or something of that sort.

'Herra's to go to her, room number (whatever it was), as soon as she comes in. I suppose she was out with you?'

'Her mother's arrival isn't going to help anyone.'

'Oh, I'm relieved that she's here.'

'You don't look it.'

She was sitting slumped on her bed; the interview with your mother had obviously been an ordeal.

'Mrs. Friedlander is taking Herra home with her to-morrow.'

'Do you really think she should be brought back where she's been so miserable, or sent to another school where she'd be less capable of surviving than ever?'

'I just can't help it, I love that child.'

Those words, so spontaneous, even a non-sequitur,

were so welcome at that moment that I took and kissed her hand.

'Then help me protect her from what happens to those who fall behind in the cut-throat struggle.'

'Are you really her friend or are you . . .?'

'Whatever words are pinned on me from the pigeon-holed depository of ready-labelled judgments, one thing, Liz; I won't add to her hurt.'

'Nobody wants to do that.'

'Did you ever see the cuttings she keeps, with phrases like "running or hounding to death" in them? That's what she's in danger of having happen to her.'

'Aren't you exaggerating a little?'

'And you, Liz, will be discarded by Mrs. Friedlander if things don't work out to her satisfaction, without a thought.'

'She blames me for Herra's defection from the group.'

'What I'm suggesting is that you come with us.'

'Her mother will never agree to your taking the child.'

'Couldn't you stop calling her "the child"?'

'That's what she is.'

'Not to me.'

'I'm shocked at what I surmise, but I think to suddenly part her from you now would lead to another of her emotional crises.'

In the room next door I found you in the midst of a crisis of another kind. In trying to flush the sawdust from the cat's tray down the toilet you'd stopped up the drain.

First turn off the bath taps that you had running full blast as if there wasn't enough water about.

'The flow from the bath was helping clear the other pipe,' you explained.

'Your mother's here and waiting to see you.'

'I can't face her.

'I've seen nothing you can't face either in imagination or fact. You're a very brave girl.'

'Don't send me to her, all the same.'

'What I need is a length of wire.'

'She could keep me, lock me in; she has the law on her side.'

'That's why you can't refuse to see her.'

'Are you just going to hand me over to her?'

I got stiffly from my knees on the wet floor from where I'd been making an investigation into the mishap. I had to proceed without a hint of panic, I mean, of course, in the major, not the minor, crisis. But now it was time to take you in my arms and tell you, in an other than verbal manner, that I'd never give you up as long as there was breath in this less-than-resilient body.

'You'll have to see her, that's certain. Try to appear calm and reasonable.'

'Do I look calm and reasonable?'

'I never know how you look to outsiders; I know how you look to me and my few friends like the three poets.'

'How?'

'No more than a little *distrait*, a poem of wild fragility.'

I tried taking a quick and more objective glance at us: An old man with wet trouser knees and shirt sleeves rolled back from scraggy arms to whom a half-crazy female kid was desperately clinging.

'But tidy yourself up before going to her room.'

I accompanied you to the door whose number Liz had given me and you stood outside it gripping my hand in what, I guessed, you thought might be a long farewell. But it was only for a moment your 'heart of wax' failed you. As I turned down the corridor I heard your bold knock.

I busied myself at freeing the drain and before I'd quite finished you were back. Before you could tell me anything I saw you were near the end of your strength, when even the creature that has put up the bravest defence and kept just ahead of its pursuers senses the end is near.

'If I refuse to return with her to-morrow she'll report you to the police.'

'Look, I've fixed this bloody mess.'

I wanted to diminish the tension, even momentarily. I pressed the lever, the bowl flushed and the water in it returned to its proper level.

'While you get into bed I'll mop up the floor.'

'Oh, I couldn't with this hanging over me.'

'Couldn't?'

'Make love.'

'Show me your wrists.'

Raw and inflamed. Who—not me—had dreamt of, let alone mentioned, making love?

'We're going to look at the slides we got this morning, you from the haven of your cot, I between you and the projector.' And also the door.

This was the one thing I could think of to do with you at this crucial moment when I didn't know, and wasn't going to ask, whether your mother was already summoning the law to her aid.

I left the bathroom floor for a quieter, later moment (would there ever be one while we remained in the hotel?) and, locking you in at your suggestion, went to my room for the apparatus.

As I was assembling it, a knock on the door. A solicitor sent by your mother to read to you the relevant section of The Parents' Authority over Minors Act, 1834, who, failing to obtain access to you (the legal jargon was echoing threateningly), had recourse to the second party or culpable accessory before, after and during the act. Just before opening the door this reasonable-seeming supposition was mysteriously replaced by an irrational one of the slaughter house assistant, supporting himself by one hand on a crutch and with a knife in the other.

'Mr. Sugrue?'

'At your service,' or, anyhow, a similarly over-polite greeting evoked by relief. This someone didn't reek at the first whiff of moral disinfectant of the well-known, official brand.

'I came about the car.'

'Please sit down.'

'I'm pressed for time, Mr. Sugrue, but I could fit in a trial run right away if that suits you.'

Into the mountains to test its hill-climbing capacity? And you in bed in your leafy nightdress-day-dress in the darkened room (I'd drawn the curtains), growing more anxious minute by minute? Explain to you the change of plan? Get up again, dress, at least to the extent of shoes and knickers, and come for a drive with, if I wasn't mistaken, a funeral contractor who wanted a car for transporting well-to-do mourners to country cemeteries.

Make a show of consulting non-existent wrist watch.

'My wife should be back with it any minute. I'm sorry if I brought you here on what may turn out a wild goose chase, but you know what women are, I mean let loose in the city . . .'

I hid myself in this verbiage while awaiting his departure that took place amid an exchange of assurances about pursuing the matter further. But mind, heart and spirit couldn't be lured down from the stormy sky where they were trying to keep vigil over you, to peck at this farmyard grain.

Having escaped the trivial and time-wasting, now came the vital arranging: set up projector on table by your bed with empty bit of wall opposite, prop you with pillows, help loosely loop main fleece of your hair through elastic band at back of your neck, freeing your face from its protective veil, say short prayer, slip in frame of transparents and switch on interior light.

Christ at the well asking for a drink from the Woman of Samaria. Christ haunted and tormented by thirst, his present one, his future one that, despite his deep reserves of silence, would force the cry from the cross and, beyond and more distant, in the past and to come, the thirsts of the exhausted, harassed and about-to-be-killed.

'There's a regulation that animals can't be kept long after arrival at the slaughter house without water.'

'Where did you get that piece of information?'

'I read it and cut it out of the paper.'

The deep, cool wells of Galilee, the lake in the early mornings, making a fire to grill the fish he'd caught and boil the water the woman (not that one, another) had drawn for him the previous evening. Were those the memories that had obsessed him then?

'When?'

Had I spoken aloud? Had you guessed my thoughts? I'd said something and you wanted it plainer.

'I'm wondering what thoughts survive when pain and despair approach their climax.'

'They don't have thoughts, at least not mental ones; theirs are in the flesh and blood.'

'I was thinking of human beings.'

'Humans or animals, it's all one when they're dying.'

'Some men cling to a hope. According to the story, Christ must have hoped he'd return early one morning to the healing peace of his lake.'

'We tell ourselves stories, like mine about Lazarella creeping back to my room; that's the difference; animals don't.'

Might as well switch off the apparatus; the idea hadn't been much of a benefit.

'Why not lie down too,' you suggested.

'We're not in the loft with the ladder drawn up.'

'We can pretend we're back there, can't we?'

Yes, indeed. I couldn't but share the make-believe that, if measured by the degree of its intensity, was more real than much so-called reality.

I was stretched beside you, not under the bedclothes though, when there was a knocking in the night, or, as, woken out of our dream, I knew the next moment, in the height of the busy day. No response coming from within, the door started opening, opening, and then your mother was standing just inside it in the glare of the light she'd switched on, a harshly-lit angel of judgment.

I never recall her first words, as neither can you. We must have shut our minds to them and forgotten them immediately. When the line was cleared again she was telling you: 'Get up and go to my room.'

I hadn't known you were naked under the bedclothes until, very much without hurrying, you pushed them back, rose with an exaggerated langour, actually paused to stretch (increasing my sense of doom), found your leafy robe of many colours and several purposes, and went with it into the bathroom.

'And you, Mr. Sugrue, will you meet me downstairs as soon as you're dressed.'

I wasn't undressed, but in shirt and trousers.

'That won't take long.'

A miserable bit of defensive irony?

Your mother left and I switched off the light and hid myself, burning from mingled shame and desire, in the semi-darkness. A bright strip from the not-quite-closed bathroom door lay across the carpet. How lure you out before it was too late? Before you were dressed and your mother was back banging on the, this-time-locked, door.

'Hey, Herra, before you dress come and look at a couple of our Old Testament pictures.'

'Whatever for?'

You weren't with me; a note of surprise in your voice mingled with the sound of the toilet flushing.

Even without the projector the inopportune longing was transporting me inside the hot tent where Rachel-Leah (I wasn't distinguishing between them) has shed her robes and is sprawled on a pile of goat skins.

I tiptoed to the bathroom door and tried to keep my quick breathing in check to hear whether you were washing (a heavenly sound) or dressing (whisper of dreaded news).

You heard, or sensed, my eavesdropping and a bare arm was thrust across the lit slit to close it. I grabbed your wrist and you pulled away, dragging me after you as you retreated and only managing to slam the door when the monster was already inside with you.

'Only not there!'

'Where?'

'My wrist.'

I was clutching you wherever I could, snapping ribbons, tearing cotton, laying ravening paws on you. And you were yelling something about my turning on you like all the others. You bit one of the fingers I was covering your mouth with to try and stop you making such a row, and to the stickiness of sweat was added the glueyness of blood.

I snatched my hand away to an assault lower down where it was caught and clasped between your thighs.

Gasps, pants. Exert enough leverage to force you to kneel on the bath-mat with the rest of you forward over the edge of the tub. Beguiling positions into which to manoeuvre you were flashing before me with the vividness of the projected slides.

A decrease in the gale-force, a quick fading out of the frenzy. Wiping the blood from my face with a piece of damp cotton that I seemed to recognise as torn from that sacred garment of yours, I fled from the bathroom.

Silence, darkness, desperation; an Ishmael condemned by you, beast and God.

I started putting away the transparents and dismantling the projector (straws to clutch at in drowning). Looking up from what I was fumbling over in the semi-dark, you were standing in the lit doorway, fully dressed and looking for something in your handbag.

I won't say I dropped on my knees before you; my joints were too stiff. I got awkwardly down on them, touched the hem of the garment that my misery had made holy and said: 'Please, please, for the true love of Christ, forgive me!'

I waited, for the axe to descend, for a last-minute reprieve.

You bent and touched the top of my bowed head with your mouth and, though my white hair is still thick, a warm tear percolated to my scalp.

'What have I done? Tell me where I've hurt you?'

'You haven't hurt me.'

'I made you feel like a small, harassed, hunted animal.'

'Oh, no, no! Just a little bitch that scratches and bites when she doesn't happen to feel like it.'

SIXTEEN

Your mother was waiting in the hall, but I couldn't see anyone, in or out of uniform, who looked as if he had been summoned to hear her complaint.

'I expect you know a place for lunch where we'd have more privacy to talk than here,' she said.

A ruse to get me out into the street where I could be apprehended without unwanted publicity for the hotel?

'If you can eat Italian food.'

'I've asked for a taxi.'

'I'll fetch the car; taxis are hard to come by at this hour.'

She came with me to where it was parked (not wanting to let me out of her sight?). We passed a guard on traffic duty on the way to the restaurant and I half-expected her to tell me to stop for her to make her accusation while pointing to my scratched face and bitten finger.

Do I have to tell *you* that whoever has once had the hue-and-cry behind him and again hears, or thinks he hears, the distant horn, is beset by dark imaginings?

A critical moment after parking the car when I was addressed by a traffic warden (with an expression of admiration for the ancient Rolls, as it turned out).

At last we were seated at a table in Manzini's, a haunt

of mine in days gone by, and a strange waiter was placing the familiar menu in front of us.

I studied your mother's face as she glanced down the card; nothing to be clearly discerned there (on her face, that is).

'One Ravioli Bolognese and a Porchetta.'

'The Porchetta's not on.'

I pointed to the item on the menu where I'd have found it blindfold. The waiter snatched it away and scrawled the name of the dish through.

'Hey, don't do that; this is the permanent card.'

Yes, that's how I'm apt to react to dangerous situations; instead of lying low I actually draw attention to myself gratuitously.

'It's off.'

'It's never off. May I speak to *le patron*?'

'Who?'

The old habitué, favoured-client act hadn't come off.

'Mr. Manzini.'

'He's not here.'

'Bring us a bottle of the Chianti.'

'Two Ravioli Bolognese, is it?'

'Certainly not. Just the wine until Mr. Manzini arrives.'

'Haven't you made enough trouble for one morning?' your mother asked when the waiter had gone.

Miraculously, our world wasn't ending! She'd addressed me as she might a naughty child.

'I can't have Herra and now, it seems, I can't even have the Porchetta.'

Was I so utterly bemused with relief that I thought this was funny? Or what?

Without knowing why, I was acting the old, sacked, no-longer-funny clown, taken to debauchery, with his eye on the circus proprietress's little, ringleted daughter. My finger pained, thoughts of you were hurting my head. None of this was of any account, seeing your mother was asking me where I planned to take you.

'Before we go into that I want to say that the only word for what I feel for Herra is pure adoration.'

Later, when I went to your room with the extraordinary news, your mother's attitude became explicable. You took a small, black automatic pistol from inside the top of your dress (brassiere?), where its flat sides had made no appreciable extra bulge, warm with the warmth of your breasts.

'I made it brutally clear to her there wouldn't be any messing with razor blades this time.'

'Where did you get it?'

'Can't you guess?'

'Mullen? But you weren't alone with him.'

'One of your poets.'

'They're yours too.'

I knew which and didn't ask.

'You've convinced your mother at last that you're serious.'

'What she means and what we mean by "serious" is miles apart. But as far as she's concerned the hunt is off.'

Moment when a ripple from the tidal wave of divine relief at the safe delivery of the cosmos from the womb of chaos touches the innermost nerves.

You started a sigh that turned into a yawn, a lovely, semi-luxurious yawn.

'Let's get married.'

'Married?'

Who, in God's (or any other reputable) name, would perform a ceremony that must seem to someone in public office, either in Church or State, a Witch's Sabbath ritual or Black Mass?

'In our own make-believe.'

Yes, I should have caught up quicker with your dream of exchanging your all-purpose garment for a one-occasion luxury (hadn't it been forshadowed in your yawn?) like a piece of wedding gear that you were ready to go and buy there and then.

What about money, would I give you some? Would I give you a warm draft of blood, had you needed it, drained from a vital organ into the tooth glass in the bathroom?

I recommended a department store where you'd get what you wanted with the least fuss and fewest questions, a hint that you were buying the regalia for a sister whose physical condition made it embarrassing for her to come up from the country and appear in person would suffice.

When you'd gone I went to talk to Liz whose fate was more than ever in the balance.

She was sitting playing patience as if the year was 1910 and she'd an idle half-hour to spend before being summoned down by gong to the evening meal with the rest of the large and cosily-united family. She was living out, for possibly the last moments before the blow fell one of her favourite make-believes.

But the spell was broken; I caught the last of the dreamy shadows on her face as they fled.

'Please tell me what has been arranged.'

What is the verdict? Or perhaps she thought she knew that and was asking for news of the sentence.

'Mrs. Friedlander has withdrawn her opposition to Herra associating with me.'

Why on earth the formal jargon?

Because, I suppose, I saw this as the first, and probably only, opportunity to solemnly announce our make-believe betrothal or even make-believe (I'm using the term in the same sense as you and the young poets do, to indicate reality as viewed imaginatively) marriage.

'I'm astonished.'

'So was I, at the time. Now that we're free to go north in the morning without being under a cloud, I want you to come with us.'

'As what?'

'As the one person Herra will let educate her.'

Liz started to weep. That's to say, she sat upright on the side of the bed with the cards that she'd swept from the bedspread in a loose pile on her lap and her shiny-wet eyes brimmed drops over her puffy face.

'Did Mrs. Friedlander mention me?'

Had she?

'I think so.'

'Did she wonder what would become of me?'

'What will become of you and us is helping each other and a few others to lead a better kind of life.'

'I'm too old.'

'What about me?'

I took one of her hands and held it between mine and, do you know, Herra, it was as vulnerable and as much needing reassurance as one of your small creatures rescued from a predator.

'It's all all right, or as right as need be. It's hard to say what I mean, we haven't got a private line going yet between us. But here we are still at liberty, alive and dependent on each other. How's that for a start?'

'I'm anxious, Mr. Sugrue. Do you know, Sugrue strikes me as less of a misnomer for you than Fintan?'

'Then call me that without the prefix.'

'Yes, I'll come with you, I haven't much choice, have I? But it doesn't look so rosy as you make out.'

'You were consulting the cards?'

'Not in the way you mean; they tell me what's already at the back of my mind where the wisest thoughts are hidden.'

'About whether you should come with us, is that what you wanted to get clear?'

'I was trying to think out what was best for Herra.'

'She really does mean a lot to you.'

'I told you.'

'What you saw was bad for her?'

'I'm not sure. Some things are beyond me, I'm not a clear-thinking woman; I wasn't even good at my job, as you must have guessed.'

Something strange, Herra: she sat there, the tears had stopped, and she struck me as having a deep, calm acceptance of everything, or even whatever she'd 'seen' from the cards. If Nancy came back from the grave she'd be like that, if any of the dead returned they'd have learned that utter patience.

As I was going she said: 'I don't know about the new life you mentioned but in my own small way I'll turn over a new leaf.'

She laid her hand on my arm, a timid, trusting touch, trusting (was it?) you to me against her will.

SEVENTEEN

I wasn't long back in my room before the prospective customer who'd called earlier about the car was back again. I explained that as I was waiting for an important telephone call (you were to ring through from your room when all was ready) I couldn't take him to the car right away.

This time he wasn't in a hurry, if it really was the same person as before; I still wasn't certain, my memory for all except a few faces is defective, but he said, as I think the earlier caller had also mentioned, that he was a funeral contractor.

'I've a Rolls hearse, beautiful 1928 job, and am looking for something stylish to match as first car for distinguished mourners.'

Yes. Better the mobile cell in which I'd prayed, speeded, sinned and suffered, being driven soberly in its latter years than desecrated by cigar-smoke and ribald laughter.

In the beginning, when Adam fell into the trancelike sleep and woke to find Eve, fact and dream were one. After the Fall the divide between reality and imagination, which for you, darling, never really operated, set in. This thought flashed between two other drab ones concerned with the car.

'I ought to tell you, perhaps, it's in two shades of grey.'

'No problem, a spray of paint will deal with that.'

When the intercom phone buzzed I told you about the prospective buyer and you said to show him you before the car. Oh, I grasped all right that for you, as in the parable, it was a matter, in the absence of wedding guests, to collect from the byways anyone to whom you could show yourself.

On the way to your room I paused to make some introductory remarks about a wedding and, I think, bridesmaids, so that the glimpse of you, which I'd decided was all he'd have, would fit the vague suggestion of coming nuptial festivities without pinpointing your role in them.

When I opened the door your mother was what I believe is called 'putting the final touches to the nuptial veil'. Of course, that wasn't what I noticed first but I concentrated on it while recovering from the shock of the sight of you in the wedding finery that had stunned and sobered me to the point of pain.

At the crucial moment (but how many crucial, incredible moments weren't part of that last, late flowering?) I had to explain about the intruder whom you were regarding with alarm.

I'd expected I wouldn't be able to keep my mind on the car and the business in hand, but as soon as I caught sight of it on the other side of the street I was filled with distress. The long, and mostly unhappy, history of the ancient Rolls came back to haunt me in a way I could never have foreseen. There were long drives with Nancy over what seemed perpetually wet roads, whither and whence I no longer knew, and, when I now opened the door, did the air really smell of tears and tobacco (she had been an incessant smoker)? I recalled journeys with

Peter to or from the various schools, all sorts of incidents binding me to the car as the monk is bound to the cell where the intensities of his inner life have been lived.

A last look-round the familiar nooks and crannies, back and front, coming on odds and ends that evoked the, until then, three-quarters forgotten: an old race card, an empty brandy flask (that I unstoppered and sniffed), a broken rosary of Nancy's, an ink-stained copy-book.

Instead of a sales talk, I made a few sober understatements about the care with which the vehicle had been kept. I was silent while the prospective buyer talked about growing competition and, I think, the decline in demand for old-fashioned funeral pomp.

'I could fit in a trial run this evening if that suits you, Mr. Sugrue.'

Nothing suited me but a speedy return to where I'd left you with the hope that I'd never have to leave you again. But I agreed and the hour (which? I wasn't sure when you asked me apprehensively) was fixed.

We shook hands (O God, do I hear you groan, get on with the real story!) and I crossed the street, entered the hotel and took the lift. And what do you think? I was so intent on hurrying back to you before one of the possible disasters that I never got to close enough grips with actually to name (an empty room, the revolver having been confiscated by a trick and you forcibly taken to the airport under police guard?) that I knocked on a door that wasn't yours, blind to the wrong number.

Christ! who was this crony in a beach-suit-bath-robe?

'What is it? Who on earth are you?'

She it was asking *me*. Lightheaded, intoxicated with fear and expectation to the point of lunacy, I announced: 'Captain Erasmus. There's a fire in a storeroom; guests are advised to descend to the foyer with their valuables.'

A headlong rush down to the right floor and, cutting the incidental commentary, I'll now record the signal that indicated I'd reached the epi-centre of shock: 'Want to take me out of this?'

You were asking this (asking!) as soon as I was inside the room.

'What?' Lay a hot hand on all that ethereal whiteness, foam of lace and silk, get my fingers into folds of softly shining . . .? 'Where's . . .?'

'My mother? Gone to cash some travellers' cheques.'

'But you've only just put it on.'

'So that we can do in style what we made a hit-or-miss job of this morning!'

I had a glimpse in the long mirror in front of which you were standing of the girl-bride being waylaid and stripped of her wedding dress by the crazed old tramp. Pale to the point of swooning, she was pleading with the drunken brute in the mirror-world; in this one she was murmuring: 'Not that hook, this one. . . . What a lot of leaves before you come to the heart of the cauliflower.'

Once out of the slim, white cocoon, your hips were twice as brown and wide as I remembered them and your thighs branched out from the trunk with the phoenix nest dark in their fork.

'We'll have to make it short; she won't be long.'

Not long, not more than all the crucial moments rolled into one, just time for what there's neither word nor rhyme for, what can be mimed but never said.

You were out of my arms and the next moment, squatting on the bidet and saying something about no dilly-dallying I couldn't quite catch for the noise of flushing. All the same, after a quick rub with a pink towel and a dab of talcum, I saw you hesitate between starting to dress and getting back on the bed with me.

Wiser councils, as the politicos put it, prevailed, and while you were getting into your two basic garments, both white with a lingering reflection of the discarded wedding dress, you said your mother was giving you money to make you financially independent of me and able, when the time came, as she put it, to escape.

'What will she think when she sees you've changed back so soon into your old dress?'

'She has stopped thinking as far as I'm concerned. Know what she said when I came in with the wedding things and asked her to help get me into them? That I hadn't matured mentally since I was nine or ten while physically I was, if anything, over-developed.'

'You don't think there could still be a hitch?'

'Surely you know that there's nothing in the way of catastrophe that I don't imagine? Each time you leave this room I think it may be the last I'll see of you.'

'Should I stay here with you when she returns?'

'It would be harder to tell her the kind of lies I have to in your presence. What I'd like if there's time, we'll risk it, is to say one of our psalms together.'

In case Mrs. Friedlander arrived back accompanied by two officers of the law with a warrant for your return to her custody, and this was our last moment or two together?

We sat on the bed we'd just been stretched out on and recited a canticle of which I was incapable of taking in more than a vague, though powerful, impression of dark lamentation shot through with flashes of hope.

PART TWO

EIGHTEEN

A disused station, a small but once-busy terminus of four platforms, waiting- and refreshment-room, booking office, book stall and offices. Not the main station which still functioned across the river but a secondary one that had served a remote and 'backward' district and that was situated in what had become one of the 'no-go' areas of the town. This was the, at first sight, not very promising looking complex of dilapidated buildings entrusted to me by Mullen and the Committee of Five who administered this barricaded district to make into a community centre, in the hope, I guessed, that I'd think of something better both to call it and to do with it.

In case I should later think I hear you ask: What about the car drive, why did you leave that out? I'll mention that it was a unique journey, being the only one we ever took together. And there were the glimpses of holy places as we passed, windows through trees, half-hidden porches, places rooted in the motionless quietude that formed banks on each side of the swiftly-flowing road. You saw them too, perhaps before I did, but you didn't enquire why we couldn't get Mullen to stop and let us out with the suitcases, the cats' basket, the fish and their aquarium so that with the money for the Rolls and what your mother had left with you we could have looked around for a safe retreat. As you put it later in all innocence: 'Mary didn't say to Jesus at the tomb: Let's call it a day; I've a friend with a house on the lake who'll lend us the top floor.'

Just once you took my hand and held it (with Liz we were at the back, Mullen had a young man I took to be his bodyguard beside him) and with your other drew my head back when I'd turned it for a last glimpse of a thatched roof at the end of a leafy lane.

The first night in the Laggan we stayed with Mullen and his wife in a small two-storeyed house whose windows, like most of the others in the row, had been broken and were partially boarded up.

We were given the three bedrooms that made up the upper floor, Mullen and his wife moving down to sleep in the sitting room. So far so good, and even the view from the part of my window that was still glazed of a wide, desolate space strewn with burnt-out cars from temporary barricades wouldn't have worried me hadn't it been for the stray animals, dogs, cats, and a lean goat, roaming the waste ground.

I imagined you at your window before you undressed, sharing, in the way I knew of but couldn't quite grasp, their plight. That is, if yours was the other front room next to mine, Liz having been allotted the larger one at the back.

Through the dividing wall I heard a clink of glass or china and the splash of water poured from the jug that must be a replica of the one in my room standing in its matching basin on a washstand.

Had you pulled the curtain without looking out and were you tranquilly washing yourself? More likely transferring the fish from the bowl in which they'd travelled to the larger tank. What you were doing became a matter of such life-and-death concern that I listened with my ear to a bunch of wall-paper roses and louder than the watery sounds heard my own quickened heart-beat. With my chest touching the wall I imagined the echo penetrating it and that the silence that now seemed to have fallen over the next room meant that you too were listening, waiting and, perhaps, yes perhaps impatiently, for me to come to you.

Start thinking these thoughts and there's no end to them; the only end to what begins as a smouldering kind of wonder about you and soon flares into a smoky, blinding wanting is in your arms.

I took off my shoes, slipped out onto the landing, slid my feet over the boards that I could tell were creaky ones (I could tell all sorts of things in this state of heightened physical consciousness) and opened what should have been the door to . . .

Liz, part-undressed, was kneeling by the bed saying her prayers. Her big face turned to me with the pallor on it that had gathered there while hidden in her hands. Better have looked on her physical nakedness than that, or was my shame exaggerated by my disappointment? Shamed and humbled at another revelation of my being subject to possession to the point where I dwell in a world of only a single street and that made up of brothels, so different to the one we share where reality is a complex mosaic of various shades of fear, love and anguish.

And now back to the disused station premises which I'd already started on when you interrupted me. At first glance the outlook wasn't much of an improvement on that from the Mullens' house. The walls were still plastered with posters of once sunny beaches, golden elixirs, seductive attire, over which the sands of the surrounding desert had now drifted.

'What's that?'

We were standing in the middle of the former waiting room and Mullen had gone through a door and was opening up what had been the refreshment room. I hadn't caught your murmured remark.

'We could replace all these lying advertisements with simple true ones. It would be a start and wouldn't cost much.'

'What sort of things?'

'Things we'd remind each other of after these vulgarities have been covered or torn down.'

'Such as?'

'You must know that better than I do. At first we might just have silence and bare painted walls and a sigh of relief. And perhaps just three words stencilled across them: *Douceur*, *volupté*, *bonheur*.'

'Except that the people here don't speak French.'

'You know what I mean.'

'Yes, Herra, I do.'

I was listening attentively. Nobody but you had such good ideas.

'A sigh of relief and then the other sigh at the thought of small, beautiful, hunted creatures.'

'How would you get that across?'

'Show them things they hardly know anymore: the natural camouflage of these creatures, the mottled coat of a hare, the speckled breast of a thrust and the coloured dots on a trout.'

At the end of the tour Mullen took us up to a second floor that had once been the station-master's quarters.

'Not that he used them in latter times and, as you see, there's a lot of work to be done to make the rooms habitable.'

But we were looking from a window and what we saw was so unexpected and healing (your word) that if the place had been twice as dilapidated we'd still have been anxious to move in.

The rows of small houses of the Laggan stretched along the ridge of one of the hills over which the town was built and, like a medieval castle, the station commanded one side; we were looking down above a steep slope of grey roofs to another more luminous expanse of grey. For a moment I couldn't get the bearings and it was you who exclaimed: 'Look, an estuary right under our window!'

'I hope you're not sorry you came now that you've seen it,' Mullen was saying.

'It's wonderful.'

Though he'd spoken to our backs, I knew that it hadn't been you he'd addressed and, as we turned, he looked at me.

'It's as she says.'

His glance (from me to you and then back) struck me as belonging to the kind of looks I'd intercepted before but couldn't immediately interpret. It took me a moment to place it among the dawning expressions of displeasure on the faces of those who have just grasped something they'd have preferred not to. Mullen had wanted to leave the problem of why we'd been (I'd been) so ready to accompany him into a desolate, embattled urban area like the Laggan and now an answer he hadn't sought was being supplied.

As we walked back through narrow streets littered with

what the ebb tide of rioting had left there a roar and rattle was resounding from the roofs. Mullen took no notice and I didn't ask him what it was until he stopped in a doorway and, with a hand on our shoulders, impelled us further into the narrow hall. It was you who answered: 'Sounds like an aerial lawn-mower clipping the clouds.'

There was a deafening clatter as if another load of scrap metal was being dumped into the street from on high. The lad with Mullen, who'd sat beside him in the car and taken turns at driving, had stepped into the street and was staggering under the impact of a gleaming brown pistol held tight to his shoulder while the black, upended barrel jerked out a jet of bullets at the helicopter.

Later that day we got together some bits of furniture donated by Mullen's and other households in the vicinity and had them transported to the station by truck. Liz was staying a few more nights where she was until we had the living quarters in some kind of shape.

We were together and free for the first time, cast up together on a deserted island as the sun set over a wide ocean, come after a long and perilous trek to an uninhabited building in a wasteland where within ancient walls that kept out the encroaching sand we walked in the evening shadows through our rose garden.

All was there in your make-believe reality. After we'd worked on one of the three upstairs rooms we strolled along the departure platform to where it ended in reddish sunlight that slanted in under the broken canopy onto clusters of flowering weeds. This was the main street of our desert city, the other three we'd explore later. Now it was time to enter the doorway still marked 'Station Master. Private' and prepare supper on the stove for which we fetched fuel from a wagon at the goods siding for which Mullen had given me the key. On a dusty shelf I discovered a Continental Train Guide some of whose tables you read out (even with my glasses I could only decipher the small print with difficulty), giving us the peculiar, imaginative thrills that I'd only have expected from certain fictions or poetry.

'Listen. A local train leaves Köln, platform 9B (I know the station well, it overlooks a busy street with a tall hotel and the Rhine at one end of it) for Krefeld every evening, winter and summer, at 8.12. That's about now, but at this time of year it's just getting dark there.'

What a strange excitement in thinking of these punctual events happening all over Europe, coinciding with this private event of having our supper here with the cats exploring the unknown room between sketchy mouthfuls from the familiar enamel plate brought from the cottage!

Returning from the ladies' toilet you asked me to come and see some graffiti you'd discovered there. On the damp-stained white wall of one cubicle was scribbled in pencil:

'Here's to the bird of love
That flies above,
May it never lose a feather
Till you and I my (word indecipherable) dove
Are tucked up in bed together.'

I read it out.

'You've altered the second word of the last line.'

It wasn't easy to read and I'd given it the benefit of the doubt.

'It's probably a quotation from a respectable poem by someone like Robert Burns.'

You were pointing to another inscription: 'I'm dreaming of a long, long fuck.'

'Isn't it refreshing? A pity they have to be hidden away in toilets and places.'

'Would you like them up in public view?'

'Oh yes, instead of the sickening ads. Be honest, wouldn't you?'

'On yon bonny brae o' heather
I'd lay doun my head and die.'

'Of shame? Why, you'd be delighted. So would most people, after the first shock. They'd breathe more easily and there'd be more laughing and less sniggering.'

'You mean we should provide space here for anyone who wanted to write up his or her sexy fantasies and imaginings openly?'

NINETEEN

The days flew by in constructing our desert city which was, however inappropriately, how we thought of it because of the novel I'd been working on a long time already and parts of which I'd read to you.

(I've heard since that the imagination sometimes shapes life as well as art, and that Kafka in 'Der Prozess' had for theme the process of disease and called down on himself the tuberculosis that killed him, and that Mahler with his 'Kindertotenlieder' caused the death of his own child.)

I'd given, provisionally, this title to the book that was set in a town hundreds of miles from anywhere, reached only by a path through a huge forest or a track across a vast desert half obliterated by sand storms; its location was not precisely defined.

Liz had rejoined us and, more for her sake than yours, I insisted on your resuming an abbreviated course of lessons with her. Mullen looked in occasionally, he'd provided us with a carpenter and plasterer, to see how we were getting on.

I saw that you didn't much like, or rather trust, him. But it wasn't the time to start you on your nervous questioning and I discouraged discussion of Mullen and the possible divergencies of his and our plans. This was easy with so many other things of immediate urgency to talk of. For instance, possible slogans to put up in place of the advertisements:

'There is no authority on this earth that is valid except that of those with no personal axe to grind, no position to safeguard. That is, those about to die.'

Somewhat too long, not incisive enough.

'I too have suffered
Obscurity and derision
And sheltered in my heart of hearts
A light to transform the world.'

Derek Mahon.

A genuine counter-current, but hardly tough enough as a slogan for all weathers and all hours.

A reproduction of the lean, ghostly Christ of the early ikons, a picture of the startled head of a wild hare, a photograph of the fat cardinal, with the caption: Which of these doesn't belong with the other two?

The hours of deepest response to our new situation came of an evening when the workmen were gone, Liz was up in her room, and the special kind of silence that we'd noticed at first over the abandoned station descended again as we took our evening stroll along the platforms. It was the silence that I tried to get into the novel: I imagined it as present in desert cities at night, on desert islands, in the cool of the evening in the legendary Garden.

Our original idea of the loft as a haven had shifted and widened, and it was you who put it best.

'The old and the tired are the ones I'm thinking of;

of course, the animals too.' And you told me something you'd seen a few evenings after the disappearance of your ginger cat when you'd been at the supper table with your mother and the guests who were always there.

'I'd a view of the houses on the other side of our road and because I was always watching for Lazarella anything that wasn't the usual coming and going caught my eye. It was an old man going up each short drive, past the smooth lawns with their revolving sprinklers, and up to the doors and then being out of the gate again almost before I'd swallowed the next mouthful.

'I was all nerves, as you can guess, and I felt his tiredness and the little store of hope that he'd set out with dwindling each time he was out on the roadway again. As mine was dwindling, though of course more slowly, too.

'I thought of you. He was more shabbily dressed than you'd been when you visited us, though not all that much. He was about your age and, in the distance, could have been you if, twenty or thirty years ago, you'd picked the wrong pellet out of the hat, except that you don't limp.'

'A limp could be part, the least, I dare say, of what you call picking the wrong pellet.'

And Liz. She hadn't ended up with the most sought-after one.

'No,' you said. 'No, she hasn't.'

But for you Liz wasn't the old man or the strayed or hunted creature.

One evening in her room that also had a view over the sometimes shining, sometimes opaque as a grey-and-black striped cloth hung out in the evening to dry, estuary, she spoke of her marriage.

'At first there was tenderness, trust and honesty. Then

for a time there was still honesty, and sex and quarrels. You know what I mean? (I did.) But in the latter years no more quarrels or honesty, a quiet kind of life for Anton with me not asking him any more questions about anything important.'

It could have been Nancy, if she had been less fiercely reserved, recounting the phases of our marriage to a friend.

'You'd have sooner the quarrels, even the violent ones?'

'Do you know, Sugrue, how terrible a quiet life with someone you love can be if the quietness is based on deceit and betrayal?'

'How well I know it, for I was he who came home and forestalled any questions, didn't notice dark looks, was the easy, unanxious one. That was when the time for "having it out", for rows and reconciliations, even for shared miseries, was past, and one of the two was what he called breathing freely again.'

'What about your wife?'

'She must have dreaded the quietude that she couldn't or daren't break, and the calmer the surface the more frightened and lonely she felt.'

'Could she have been as fearful as I was? And am often still.'

'She got ill and died, but you're here with a life ahead.'

'Isn't she better off?'

'The dead have no future; that's so obvious it doesn't need saying, but when I think of some of them who were close to me I can't quite get it into my head.'

'Herra doesn't want me here, I'm in the way.'

'She wants what I want, as long as I want it strongly enough. And that's you sharing what we call living with us, that the dead can't anymore.'

She turned her big, pallid face to the window.

'Be patient and trusting, Liz.'

What was she looking, or listening, for? Undertones? As she'd come not to trust what the man she'd loved most said to her or had tried to catch in the undertones an echo of the old tenderness.

But there was something else on her mind.

'Because I've nowhere else to go I shut my eyes to what's going on right under my nose. That can't turn out well, Sugrue, to condone wrong-doing for the sake of what suits me.'

'You're no longer responsible for Herra; Mrs. Friedlander didn't even know whether you were coming with us.'

'You share a room with her, you don't even hide it!'

'Don't you know that she's nobody else but me and that I won't ever harm her? Must you still stick to the old hard-and-fast rules and regulations? They haven't worked all that well, have they?'

I was putting questions for her later to put to herself.

As if to help her find the answer, at breakfast the next morning the spoon went through the shell of the egg you were eating and you burst into tears.

'Herra, what is it?'

Liz, who hadn't taken in the small contretemps, supposed, I believe, that you were overcome by the realisation of the accumulated shamelessnesses of the nights spent with me.

'They're paper-thin.'

'What is; what are, darling?'

The diaphragm? The torn web of innocence?

'The wretched creatures in their crowded cages are so exhausted and half-crazy that, with the music blaring all day long, they don't know what they're doing. Instead of forming the wonderful little capsules, properly constructed to shelter new life inside them, almost shell-less eggs role out of them until they sicken of the abscesses all over their livers and they're pulled out of the batteries like broken-down machines and thrown into the incinerator. I've got the clipping about it here somewhere.'

You opened your hand-bag and a few last tears dropped into it.

'We'll turn one of the old wagons into a hen-house and wire in a run between two platforms.'

'And rear chicks?'

On one of our rare expeditions outside the Laggan, first passing the barricades manned by members of the revolutionary movement and then, proceeding in file, between the wall of a burnt-out house and the neatly-piled sandbags of a military outpost, we'd noticed a pet shop incongruously open in a street of boarded-up shop windows. It was back there that you took me to see what could be got in the way of tin hoppers or feeding troughs with which to furnish the goods wagon (the carpenter could make nests and perches).

Once outside the Laggan we were back in what to you was the hostile world, though in that part of it where the conflict was open, with a series of nightly bombings, shootings and exploding gas canisters.

You interpreted what was happening in your own way and I didn't try to explain it in more generally accepted terms, none of which seemed adequate. The soldiers on patrol, strolling with an exaggerated casual slowness through the streets in their jungle camouflage, lounging along with weapons tucked, as if casually, under their arms, the weapons themselves strange-looking, elongated implements. You were reminded, you said, of people at a winter resort in their ski-suits and burdened with their apparatus.

The shop window was boarded up like the others and the interior was dimly lit so that it was hard to see what was beyond the counter. Nothing? Had the old fellow—probably not as old as I, I reminded myself with the by now familiar slight pang—who greeted us abandoned his business in despair? Was this another small corner from which the kind of life you instinctively shared had fled or been driven?

But I was sniffing the smell of small, captive creatures and listening to a faint rustling.

Anywhere else you'd have expected me to 'do the talking' but here you were asking the proprietor, who had turned from another customer as we entered, about what you needed without any prompting.

'What's that?'

A grey shadow was crouched on the counter under the young man's hand whose fingers moved through the fur on each side of the wedge-like head, the palm, as I could now see, over the long flat-laid ears.

'Found her in the yard of a burnt-out house.'

'But what . . .?'

'A Belgian hare, Miss.'

You hadn't been here long enough to distinguish our various island accents from those that gave the language another tone.

'It looks like a wild one.'

'I know; but we breed them at home; other kinds too, come to that.'

'Lucky hare, then, that it was you found it.'

'Not so lucky, I'm afraid, Miss. No place for her in barracks, that's why I'm here.'

'She's trembling.'

'I'd say she's due anytime.'

'Due for what?' you asked in quick alarm.

'For leverets. Feel.'

Did he take your hand with his free one and guide it to the creature's underbelly whose paler gleam I caught?

I was looking and not looking, at the counter in the dim shop and at the cottage the day of your first coming there; you were holding the rescued creature to your breast.

Your head was bent lower over the counter, not, as I first thought, to examine the hare but to write something the young man was telling you on a scrap of paper supplied by the shop owner. Instructions for the care of a doe in kindle (I learnt this word later from the paperback you'd bought at the shop)? But that was lore you'd have absorbed without need of written reminders.

As we left the shop with you carrying the cardboard box in your arms, you explained that you'd noted down his address in case of an emergency. Don't ask: What emergency? Nor: What address? These answers I knew or guessed. But did you realise who or what the young man was?

'A soldier. Look.'

You indicated the slip of paper squeezed in one of your hands holding the box which I extricated and read: 'Sergeant George Hide, Mintona Barracks,' with a telephone, and extension, number.

The walk back was the nearest so far of all our 'outings' to a mini-Calvary. It took two minutes and the first terrified glances for me to grasp that you couldn't have been carrying a better imitation of one of the devices that were causing all the havoc.

Reports on our progress having no doubt been radioed to the nearest army post, a Ferret armoured car screeched up beside us as we turned into the steep winding, half-demolished street that led home. Before it had stopped I saw, as under a bright light with the rest of the room in darkness, the point of thread as it slips through the eye of the needle, and saw nothing else, the muzzle trained on us from the slit.

A shouted order to drop what you were carrying. Which I repeated to you without haste; that's how fear takes me, slowing me down even more, congealing me into pseudo-calmness.

'Can't; there's a sick animal inside.'

Two soldiers had jumped out and it was them you addressed.

'See for yourself.'

You opened the flap a couple of inches. White face inclined, eyes clear with resolution, dark with the knowledge of the vulnerability of what you bore, as Beatrice her innocence, through the infernal region.

Did one of the soldiers look into the box? I don't know; my senses were recording some details and not others according to a scale of their own as to which were vital and which were not. Remarks were exchanged between the soldier on the pavement with the weapon, itself like a strange, captive creature, reptilian, still gleaming with the wetness of its natural element, in the crook of his arm, and the driver of the car.

Against all my expectations, we were walking on. We hadn't been told to stay where we were or been searched, nor ordered into the vehicle.

'Before we get to the army post at the end of the street you'll have to take it out and hold it in your arms.'

Somebody else (but somebody was never you) would have objected. How keep a grasp on the terrified creature? You nodded.

The doe, supported on a forearm and firmly covered by the other, lay flatter than I thought it could have made itself, a hare-skin you were wearing on your breast. We filed through the narrow passage, traversed the littered waste to the second barricade, manned by a couple of youths, one in the customary black beret, the other wearing the old steel helmet you'd loaned him when, helping us carry our belongings from Mullen's to the station, he'd admired it.

TWENTY

Saturday night: time of week when the level of violence in the town below rises, explosions rattling the windows which were usually open to lessen the chance of being broken but that tonight you had closed against the seepage of C.S. gas. Rifle and automatic fire, use of both high and low velocity weapons being distinguishable, as reported in the news media, but to return to my exclusively private report: you clung to me and murmured: 'Imagine if the sergeant hadn't noticed the doe.'

'Start imagining, darling, and it's goodbye to any chance of sleep.'

Not that sleep came in question, still less love-making. Below the noise of hostilities you were listening to faint rustlings from the improvised hutch, anxious, I knew, because the doe hadn't settled.

To the sounds of war from outside and those of disquiet from close-at-hand was added a carefully opened door and the pad of feet across the bare boards.

'For Christ's sweet sake!'

'It's only me.'

Both bedrooms had doors to the hall, but the kitchen was a cul-de-sac only reached through ours.

Liz was cold, her feet were frozen, was there such a

thing as a hot-water bottle for which she could heat a kettle of water? Or was she just plain scared by the mini-battle a few streets away?

'Let her look for the bloody thing herself.'

There was nothing for it, though, than to look where I thought I'd seen such a utensil at the back of a cupboard.

In the tiny, bright kitchen her face, close to mine, looked drained of blood, indeed of life, with the normally-covered blue shadows exposed around the eyes and mouth. She had on a woolly bed jacket over her pyjamas.

I found the hot-water bottle and put on the kettle.

'I'll see if it leaks.'

I might have tested it straight away but had an idea that hot water would find small punctures in the possibly perished rubber that cold mightn't penetrate.

We were so close that small movements had to be co-ordinated as in dancing. I was conscious of what was bottled-up beneath the soft wool of the bed jacket and behind the long grey-green glance that she gave me. I touched her hand; it was like loosening a too-tightly turned tap.

'Wouldn't it have been better, Sugrue, if . . . I mean more suitable and *convenable* . . .'

'If I had you instead of Herra?'

'I can say it now because it's too late, as far as the girl's concerned, the harm is done.'

'The harm was done long ago, Liz, and, as I've told you, not by me. It's only I can help her. Otherwise, there's sense in what you say. Basic sexual urges aren't all that hard to satisfy; there are refinements and luxuries in picking and choosing, but that's all.'

Would the bloody kettle never boil?

Oh, I may as well say it: I could have fucked her then and there!

'It would have done her good,' was your comment. You were right. Liz would have responded with the shuddering shock of wonder and relief of the starved and lonely. 'What stopped you?' you asked a day or two later when we'd time to discuss it. Hard to find a word except the suspect one too much in evidence in too many questionable places: on slips of paper tucked into bunches of roses, on In Memoriam, Birthday and other cards.

Fill the rubber bag, wipe dry the cloth cover, test for leaks.

'There you are, happy dreams and sweet repose. . . .'

Back in bed with you was back in the here-and-now from the long-ago shade of Nancy.

'What's wrong with her?'

'Fright, loneliness and, perhaps, the need of something to take the place of all the wine.'

'I don't blame her; she's had a terrible time, what with the way they treated her at school, taking advantage of her hangovers, being dismissed because of me, knowing what was going on between you and me and being powerless to interfere and the struggle with her alcoholism all the time as well.'

The room was quieter; the doe had settled down or, as you suggested, was by now exhausted. You asked about the measurements of the hutch you were going to ask the carpenter to make for you. The window rattled at longer intervals from the detonations, whether gelignite or petrol bomb, I couldn't yet always distinguish.

Your breathing was easier, without the tense, listening pauses between breaths. 'Still, still to hear her tender-taken breath. . . .' Did I murmur aloud? Your limbs relaxed like those of a body unbound from the stake, you were loose in my arms.

The more exhausted you were the more you dreaded saying good night and closing the interior door between us to find yourself alone in the haunted room of your mind.

Anything served to keep the door ajar: fragments of ditties or nursery rhymes from your childhood (not all that far away!).

'Know what the cave said to the wave? Fill me with foam!'

'Where does that come from?'

'From down here.' You took my hand, as you had long ago (long? A few days) and laid it on the sunny, polished, subtly-convex, marble top of your belly.

As I've no doubt said, your make-believes were as real to you, more real, than the untransformed experiences of most of us.

'Or don't you want to?'

I too could resort to the tactile signs that, being nature's language (O God! I hear you groan), you grasped so well. I'm thinking of the signals you picked up from animals, not of this particular case in which there was no ambiguity.

Gravity was less binding on your world of fantasy-realities, and you could take disconcerting leaps. In the intensely preoccupied moments between your ingenuous query and the simple preparations for our con-celebration, as you sometimes called it, a, to me, quite irrelevant thought had struck you.

'What a long way from "I am The Immaculate Conception" to "you sexy cunt!"'

'What of it?'

'What a wonderful range of roles there are for women!'

Close your mouth with mine; make you attend. But you turned your head sideways on the pillow.

'Can't you shut up!'

'You've put it out of my mind, what I was going to say.'

Your attention wasn't difficult, though, to bring back to where it had been a moment ago. Ah, Herra, it was always as easy to enrapture as to wound you! You were equally exposed to the winged as to the barbed arrows.

Next day you hadn't much trouble to get the carpenter to start on the hutch. You were out between the tracks beyond where the platforms ended gathering dandelions when Mullen called.

He was on a tour of inspection though he tried to make his visits seem casual. The first thing he disapproved of was one of our latest poster-slogans: 'Drugs are an excellent strategy against society but a poor alternative to it!'

'We're against drugs, you know.'

The reformer had spoken.

'But not against sport that involves the butchering of animals?' You'd heard that some of them attended coursing meetings.

'I don't see what that's got to do with it, Miss Friedlander.'

It wasn't the best sign that he hadn't got round to calling you Herra.

You were silent. You hadn't the gift of communicating to strangers the connecting links between your wide-apart thoughts. How often had I listened in misery as, to somebody who didn't understand you, you spoke in utterly misleading and clumsy words of one of your subtle insights!

I tried to explain to a not-very-interested Mullen.

'She means that everything that breathes is wonderful and those whose only pleasure in these creatures is using them in a sport that involves their terror and death reminds her of the bored citizens who went out of town on a Friday afternoon to get a thrill from watching Jesus on his cross.'

Instead of answering, Mullen asked when I thought the station could be opened. There were these young people at a loose end who never moved beyond the ghetto except to take part in throwing stones and bottles at the troops on Saturday afternoons and then retreat behind the barricades in a cloud of C.S. gas.

'We've been telling them about what you're doing and planning and they already feel they've something up here to feel proud of as an alternative to the life in the big world outside. That's why you've got to be careful in what you tell them and put up in place of the old advertisements. They're mentally starved, the thoughtful ones, and they'll drink it all in as gospel.'

Disliking Mullen one minute, holding him in some regard the next, that was the pattern. It wasn't an easy relationship, and now as we climbed the stairs to our living quarters the possibility, never far off, of a complete and sudden break in it grew.

He'd been upstairs on other occasions and had supposed, without anyone having to say so, that the double room belonged to you and Liz. But there was the danger of his catching indications of the real arrangement, such as finding Liz in obvious occupation of what should have been mine.

This time Liz actually saved the situation; she heard us coming and quickly moved from her bed on which she'd been resting to ours. But she'd left her fleecy bed jacket, that I'd been conscious of as the invitingly flimsy veil between me and her big breasts, in the kitchen last night, on her own. To remind me how much simpler it would have been had the sleeping arrangements, while appearing to be as she was now suggesting, were, in reality, as the supposedly-forgotten bed jacket betrayed? Or, this time, am *I* being too subtle?

As I get older I tend to see manifestations of an intense and often complex eroticism everywhere, whereas Mullen struck me as unaware of these all-pervading tensions generated by the most casual contacts, visual, tactile, audible, olfactory, with the feminine.

Mullen sniffed, caught a glimpse of the shadow in the crate and told Liz: 'Don't stir, Mrs. Considine; I'm just seeing how the work's getting on. What have you there, rabbits? I noticed a lot of French families kept them for eating while I was over there.'

Liz, whom he knew had been teaching on the Continent was, to him, as foreign as you, though I suppose he presumed her French because of her going to Mass on Sundays.

A brief silence, which I'm sure he didn't remark as a shocked one emanating from you.

'I thought the carpenter was up here,' Mullen remarked before we descended the stairs again.

Past some more of our slogans on the way to where the carpenter was at work in one of the former waiting rooms on the hutch.

'In a healthy society there must be a few people who think differently about almost everything, if only a few.'

'I'd omit the last four words; keep them as simple as possible.'

One up for Mullen on the score board I was keeping.

'A local train leaves Köln, platform 9B, for Krefeld at 20.12, winter and summer.'

'What are you trying to say there?'

A quick word of hopeful explanation before you confused him even more.

'Just an idea that may not come off; a reminder that though this line is closed that doesn't make the station a dead end. There are others running to schedule all over the place, between all sorts of foreign towns and cities, through warm and humid or clear and frosty evenings, over wide and shining rivers, across dark, winding streams. We've other extracts up from a Continental time-table in the canteen; it's an imaginative link with the rest of the world.'

We passed the portion of newly white-washed wall over which you'd painted in black letters: 'There's no more need to hide your fantasies in the toilet; write them here.'

Mullen noticed nothing, another indication that his sexual indifference isolated him from the casual contacts with the world of erotica that I, for instance, can't walk down a street without making. If, on the other hand, you'd written in small letters: '*Adeste Fideles*' right at the top of the wall he'd have seen them, stopped and nodded approvingly. But, as usual, I'm oversimplifying a character I don't really understand.

'Tom!' exclaimed our puritan hero on seeing the carpenter bent over his bench, giving the name an inflection that turned it into a greeting and revealing, as did his quick, short steps, the precisely-controlled high-pressure inside him.

The boy helper stiffened with pride under the hand

laid on his shoulder. In small, oblique ways I was realising what I could have learned from the papers had I read them: that Mullen had become the incorruptible revolutionary in this part of the land.

We were awaiting the fatal question, hoping it wasn't going to be put after all, and that what for us filled the foreground with pale, freshly-sawed planks and wood shavings would, like your lettering on the platform wall, escape Mullen's attention.

'What's this?'

Your heart, your heart of wax, of oak, of fire, of an incompatible mixture of components that I couldn't imagine even a creative genius combining in a functioning psychic organ. . . . I was going to say that I saw by your face that what I call your heart fell. But what I saw could as well have been the pallor of resolution.

'It's my fault, Mr. Mullen. I begged him to make me a hutch for the hare.'

TWENTY-ONE

Much later that day, after I'd managed by working non-stop to knock together a two-compartment cage or shelter out of what the carpenter, on Mullen's orders, had left unfinished, we were leaning at our window, the door locked behind us and the estuary wide with moon-light before and below.

You were begging me to tell you a story, not one of the ancient tales, which, anyhow, we'd no projector to illustrate, but one about the future. You'd been reminded of the Rhine at night and from that it hadn't been much of a leap to want me to recount the sort of day we might spend on holiday together far from this beleaguered place.

You'd got into your faded, much-washed, all-purpose garment and were dabbing antiseptic on the cuts and abrasions on my hands that had resulted from the final burst of sawing and screwing-together.

'Money is short, so we stay at your mother's and are in separate rooms. After a late breakfast with her and the usual guests we set out in the heat-scented morning. It's already hot when we spread our towel on the almost white, finely-sifted sand that, together with scraps of paper, corks, cigarette butts, all desert-putrefied, give off a faintly bitter aroma that mixes with the sexy whiff of sun lotion from prone, glistening bodies.'

'Is it just a tale about sun-bathing?'

'Be patient; there are atmospherics to think up and detours by which the central shock must be approached if it's to have any effect.'

'Go on.'

'We'd come as far as the suburban train could take us but here we were in our semi-nakedness in a semi-naked crowd, which wasn't very far in the right direction.'

'We could get into the tepid, soupy-green lake.'

'Wade in with scarcely a shiver as the water crept up our legs and over our bellies.'

'Partly hidden, press close from the waist down.'

'You half-floated, were half-supported on my forearms, lifted lightly, an offering, stretched before me on the water, hair afloat, chin back, toes tiptilted and, in between, breasts abloom beneath a scrap of cloth, belly alternately raised and awash as I gently rocked you up and down, thighs lightly closed and falling open as the water rose between at the downward dip.'

'I don't see how it could happen in the water with all the people about and the watchers on the tower with their whistle.'

'No. Not till afternoon. We're in and out of the water several times, lying in the sun needles, anointing each other with the holy oil, eating our Pascal sandwiches (it's the hot vigil of the feast) and all the time there's an ache in those muscles that have been under unrelieved pressure from your nearness, especially in the under-water contacts.'

'I get a hollow ache there too.'

'What?'

My finger was at your mouth as you were trying to suck a wood splinter from a small wound.

'At last we've been under the showers, dressed, wrung out the bathing things and are walking back towards the station through the pine wood.

'We don't say anything; we start strolling casually, and without at first noticing we've left the path, through the trees. We hardly look where we're going, we don't seem to see anything but all the same we're guided to where it's quietest, where the sound of voices don't reach us. We're ALONE.'

'Let's have a short pause, just lean on the window-sill and imagine, and then make it true.'

As, a moment later, we turned from the window the doe was lolloping to the hutch whose door, that actually worked, we'd left open with something that was dark in the moonlight in her mouth.

'What was it?'

Anxiety in your voice; an anxious moment until she emerged again from the inner shrine apparently unharmed. She sat in the shadows and with curiously ducked head tore tufts of fur from her breast.

'That's the sign the sergeant said to wait for; her time has come.'

Strange and touching sight! Doubly so to see these age-old, secret preparations being made in the narrow breathing-space between half-forgotten past perils and unrecognised ones to come.

Transported out of one into another kind of fable, you lay in bed with wet, closed eyelashes.

'If only we have some peace to-night!'

Sand, sun and scented oil, summer dress hitched high as you lay down in the pine-aromaed shade, revealing in the most ancient and ever-latest of shocks brown belly, this one still cool from the shower, shelving steeply to the fecund, subcutaneous warmth (you hadn't put on your knickers after bathing) was suddenly over and done with.

You were back where you'd been most of the day, retelling yourself old legends that, first related to you at a time when you'd been so lonely and anxious for somebody to share your pain, you'd never got over.

'The night after the Crucifixion Mary Magdalen performed as usual in the strip-tease joint where she worked but afterwards went home alone to her attic.'

You were listening to the doe as she thumped across the floor with a tuft of fur in her mouth that she had plucked from her breast.

But I wasn't so quickly to be lured back into these haunted rooms and streets and cemeteries of yours. I went on, though not aloud, with my own different fantasy.

As we reached the café near the station from which an electric train would take us back to the city, I left you on the grass verge of the road and went to the café toilet. On coming out I looked for you but you were hidden by a car that was driving off again after stopping beside you as you lay in a posture of sensual relaxation (easily mistaken, I supposed, for one of provocation by a passer-by) on the embankment.

I couldn't leave you alone for a moment on a public highway without someone inviting you into his car! Which imaginary situation was making me want to lead you back into the pine wood where, though less private and convenient than the bed we were sharing, you'd be back in the sex obsession that fear had driven you out of in the actual present.

'Before it was light, when she couldn't stick lying dressed and awake on her cot any longer, she jumped up and rushed to the grave. She thought she'd been through all the horrors and shocks and would be left to mourn in quiet, but she found it open and empty. They, his torturers and hers, had come and taken what was left away.

'In her panic she appealed to the first person she saw, though she was in awe of even minor officials such as a park-keeper or cemetery warden, as she took him to be.

'The hope of keeping this tryst had helped Jesus endure the worst hours on the cross. Do you know what those were? Not just the bodily torment, not Satan with the familiar temptations about coming down and proclaiming himself king. That was childish compared to the drowning in watery wastes where there's nothing but the nameless monster.'

I saw Melville's White Whale. And I knew the name of yours with its savage, joker's, blubbery heart that nothing could touch, not the sharpest harpoon: Moby Joe.

'Jesus had been waiting for hours, tempted to go and suddenly appear in her room; his wounds were still bleeding a little and she'd have gently let her tears fall once more on his sore and aching flesh.

'They didn't see each other again; she went on working in the night club, started singing chansons and became a hit overnight, especially with *Non, je ne regrette rien*. Later, her songs became very sombre and full of *chagrin* but they still had that passion that Jesus had recognised and commented on when they'd first met.'

Silence. After a bit I thought you might have gone to sleep but you ran your hand through my hair and asked: 'Are you still thinking about us in the wood?'

'Oh no, you managed to put that out of my head and what I've been thinking are such chilling thoughts that I couldn't make love even if you wanted it.'

'Did you sometimes think chilling thoughts with Nancy?'

'On the contrary, it was she who was chilly.'

A loud blast rattled the window and made the doe flatten herself against the floor.

TWENTY-TWO

Next morning while we were still in bed the doe emerged from the inner compartment and lolloped out of the hutch followed by what for a moment looked like a string of tiny creatures. I felt your heart stand still with a momentary fear of some awful miscarriage until we saw that what she was trailing after her was a skein of the hay with which she had woven the nest entangled in her long hind legs.

All being so far well, I took the afternoon off to visit Peter while you kept vigil in our room. It was as much the trawler as anything more personal that took me there; you know how small, sheltering enclosures fascinate me (born with an ark-complex), mobile ones in particular and, above all, as I realised when Peter showed me round, those that sailed the seas.

When I imagined these small cabins as the only human habitation in a watery wilderness each piece of furniture became a touching token of our attempt to humanise our tiny corner of the cosmos.

Seated at the narrow table in the saloon while Peter fetched the drink, what I'd supposed was the lap of small waves on the hull turned to sobbing that came from the upper bunk opposite that I couldn't see over the rim of.

By stepping on the edge of the lower one I could see a form huddled under a blanket. The dream I'd had the night before you had telephoned me at the cottage, as sometimes happens with those of no significance, was coming true. (A writer of renown might relate the two, dream and reality, in a manner that would leave one less loose thread in this narrative.) My hand, under the cover, touched a prickly, shaven head and I reflected that, after all, the similarity had been only surface.

'You'd better look out,' Peter said behind me, 'she bites.'

My hand had been taken and held in a tight but gentle grip.

'It's not a sailor's.'

'No.'

Relief, or curiosity, brought the wet-cheeked face with long-lashed eyes out of its hiding place.

'You're old!'

My freed hand rested on naked flesh.

'I wish I were dead.'

'I doubt it.'

No use her pretending she was you.

'I would, mind you, if I wasn't scared of waking all alone in the dark.'

'In the natural course of events I'll be there a good fifty years before you.'

'Where?'

'In my bunk in the dark.'

It was you I was talking to while keeping this other girl from hiding herself again under the cover.

I was continuing our speculation about Moby Joe and thinking of death as the real confrontation with him from inside the coffin-whaler.

As well as the whiskey bottle Peter had returned with several school exercise books under his arm that he placed on the table.

I relinquished my foothold to let the girl pull on jersey and jeans on the bunk.

'They've been lying about for years in a suitcase.'

Opening one of the rather tattered copy books, I recognised, even without my glasses, the rather slovenly, curiously unformed script. (Catching sight of the envelope addressed in it, hadn't it lit with a strange, pure glow a whole Christmas for me?)

Peter poured the drinks, the girl swung her legs over the edge of the bunk (she'd tied a scarf over her head) and I began to read.

'One fine September morning in the middle of the fruit season we were married in that church in Nuremburg that stands in the market place. There was mingled with the incense and the dimness of the church, the smell of grapes, of apples, of plums, the whiteness of my shimmering dress, the glow in your eyes. The church was very full because nobody had been forgotten. . . .'

There was a twittering from the top of the companionway where young, nervous faces were peering down at us.

'Clear off; I've a visitor.'

'What about Rosie queening it there, with us out in the cold?'

'Who was out in the cold all night tied to the lamp post after you'd all run away?'

'Can't we come on board till it quietens down a bit?' they appealed to Peter.

'I haven't heard a thing.'

'Not in there you don't. The shock doesn't cross water, not even the narrow strip between ship and quay.'

Young voices softened by the surplus breath between the words.

In the excitement of the exchange with them their little sister's feet were swinging across the open copy book until I took them by the big toes and held them still.

'How can I name them all from the past and present? And in a side gallery were all the beasts most beautifully behaved. . . . Then the wedding was over and we stood outside the church, my hand on your arm.'

I took a drink of whiskey from the glass I'd moved out of the way of the girl's feet, stained from the rubble they'd stepped through in sandals. On an empty stomach (like you, I hadn't eaten lunch) Peter's measure was enough to transpose a protective film over the scrawled words. (Your car has a heart like yours; protect it from unnecessary wear and tear; radio commercial.)

Not so long after Nancy had been transcribing her adolescent day-dreams I, returning from her funeral, had picked up the girl hitcher.

'How do you know it was you she imagined as her dream-bridegroom?'

I don't, and it doesn't make much difference. I saw that she went on to name all those present, including the pets that she'd mourned, but I didn't read further to find out whether I was among the guests. Let the identity of the hero of her last fantasy remain secret.

'The captain told you to fuck off,' sang out the voice from the bunk.

'I've got to go.'

'Not you!' she laughed.

'If you and the girl want to leave you can let me know and I'll have the van collect you and your belongings, including the animals. I'll be here a few days longer.'

'You mean if there's a break with Mullen?'

'Right.'

I asked Peter about Mullen.

'Two years in a clerical college, then a period with some such outfit as the Palestinian guerrillas, and back here where the fanatic, puritanic mind has always had a following on this island of schizophrenics.'

'Yet I don't really dislike him, because, perhaps, most of my hatred is expended on those whose power derives from a mediocrity that assures them wide support because, coming from the top, it confirms a lot of people in their own petty cowardices that otherwise they'd have to be ashamed of.'

'You both believe in excess, you and Mullen, you've that in common.'

On the quayside I was beset by pale, upturned, nervous faces. Driven from their half-demolished, dead-end streets in search of what one of them called a 'lift-up' or 'lift-out', the girls' dream was of a foreign sailor that gradually faded into a drug-induced one.

The last entry I had read in the copy-book: 'Our pride and peace were deeper than the starry night.'

TWENTY-THREE

As soon as I entered the room what struck me were the untouched cabbage leaves. Only after that did I take in the doe hunched up in a corner, her head dropped sideways, her eye a dull black and her fur without its sheen.

'I think the leverets are dead.'

'I'll have a look.'

I dare not show the same indecision and fear as you or we were lost even before the crisis that I sensed was threatening had descended.

I pulled back the galvanised bolt (that I'd been so proud of) on the door to the inner compartment. In the front, right-hand corner (the one furthest from the small opening to the other part of the hutch) was the nest in the straw. Nothing was visible. Then, as we held our breath, a minute rising and falling under the covering of fur. A glimpse of the secret womb of the cosmos to which I was connected by an umbilical cord whose pull I was aware of; I closed and rebolted the door.

'I'll phone the soldier.'

The telephone was in what had been the stationmaster's office; I put through the call for you and, to my surprise, in no time I heard: 'Sergeant Hide', followed by battalion number and name of regiment.

'Hold on; Miss Friedlander wants to speak to you.'

I flinched at the sound of your voice with the old distress and the new foreboding all the clearer in it now that you were speaking to somebody else.

'What did he say? Surely he's not going to try to get here?'

I'd supposed you were only going to describe the sick creature's symptoms and ask his advice.

You had put back the receiver but you still lingered at the old-fashioned, high desk with the useless time-table above it.

'When a sailor's finished with one of the girls he carries her, shocked and shivering, to his neighbour's bunk.'

'How on earth do you know?'

No point in asking, no need to tell me. Your insight into certain cruelties went deeper than any factual report.

Back in our room, I suggested going with you, or instead of you, to the barricade, but you said that would draw unnecessary attention to our visitor.

'Leave it to me; they'll think it's a boy-friend from the town I'm meeting.'

No good telling you that the couple of times a soldier in plain clothes had been found in a no-go area he'd been shot. The sergeant must know this even if you didn't.

'How much longer will the bloody girl be?'

Though I asked it aloud the question wasn't really addressed to Liz who had looked in an hour or so later to see if we were ready for the evening meal.

After the initial blasts that the water nymphs had reported it had been a quiet enough night so far. But by now I knew what I hadn't realised before: none of these nights were nights to wait for someone to come home out of. I was listening, as you had listened for Lazarella.

While I waited I watched the doe, relating its drooping head and general air of dejection to the degree of danger you were in at that particular moment. In the second that the door took to open and reveal you, followed by the sergeant, in your un-bloodstained, summer dress I took the leap back into what for our peace of mind we call the world of reality.

'Oh, the trouble I had in persuading them to let George through! Luckily all they found on him was this booklet, and that's what finally convinced them he was harmless.'

You showed me the veterinary pamphlet while George and I, as I was now calling him, shook hands. Then he was stretched on the floor beside the doe, one hand stroking the twitching snout, the fingers of the other probing the paler under-belly.

'Nothing left there; they're all out.'

'How can she feed them if she's so sick?'

That was the question you could put into words, the one about how to kill the leverets should she die, you couldn't.

Once up from the floor and seated at the table for the evening meal, George was awkward and embarrassed.

Liz, with no idea of who he was or where he'd come from, apologised for the shortage of cutlery.

'I wasn't expecting Buckingham Palace.'

He made it sound like Beckenampellis and I saw you wondered what he meant.

'They were still breathing when we peeped in earlier this evening,' you told him.

'I'll have a look.'

I think he was relieved to get away from the table. He opened the hutch and with a finger gently exposed a huddle of tiny, naked, pink-grey, fragile monsters, curled up together, disproportionately big, puckered heads fitted into the space between fore- and hind-legs of the next link in the perfect little circle.

'She hasn't been near them all day.'

'In the wild state she'd suckle them at night when she'd be less likely to be followed to the nest.'

'If she was free . . .' You broke off, appalled, I think, at realisation of all that a sick wild creature with young must contend with.

'She'd find herbs to dose herself on,' the sergeant told you.

'Can't we get some to give her?'

He said he'd drive up the estuary in search of a weed that grew near rivers.

'I'll call back to-morrow if I can make it, otherwise the day after.'

This was the promise you longed for, something to keep hope alive.

But first there was the long night; the fears that you had ways of controlling in the day there seemed no escape from but in love-making.

Just as I thought you were at last asleep a blast rattled the window and caused the doe to flatten herself against the floor. A longish silence, but no sense of reassurance. You ran a hand through my hair and the thrill that should have shot down (by way of the spine?) to my lower parts drained off before it had really got going like a rivulet into sand.

'Try to sleep, Herra.'

Hurt? Surprise? on your part. Embarrassment, resentment on mine.

'Let's get dressed.'

However unexpected your proposal, anything was

better than staying where we were. Not a word as you put on your silk blouse, mini skirt, but, I noted, no tights, and then started brushing your lack-lustre hair in what I feared was an excess of nervous energy.

'Where are we off to?'

We were halfway down the stairs before I asked, having hoped that all you had in mind was a midnight picnic in the kitchen.

'A train called "The Diplomat" leaves Bâle for Hamburg and Altona at 22.10.'

No, you hadn't recalled noticing a weed on one of the derelict sites that you'd suddenly imagined might be the curative one.

Nothing had yet been done to the platform you led me onto; its broken paving lay in almost complete darkness.

'Wait till you hear the carriage door close.'

I was still at sea as you walked off up the platform towards what I realised were a couple of ancient railway carriages abandoned at its far end.

I'm still not sure about the nature of the chemico-imaginative impulses that cause the physical phenomena that make sex work. But it wasn't going to work with me to-night. My feeling wasn't right. How could I tell before I tried? When I thought of the world around me I didn't see it primarily as a place behind whose doors and walls, in whose alleyways and woods, in whose parked cars and trains, men and women were coupling, naked or in various degrees of undress. I hadn't that key-hole glimpse through the door of outward appearance that I knew by experience preceded active sex where women, however busy in their social or business roles, became exquisitely sexual domestic animals. It's the sudden juxtaposition of the outwardly decorous to the secretly and shamefully indecorous that sparks off the inner combustion that ignites the senses.

So there you are, darling; I hope I've made it clear why our little act was doomed to fail before it got properly going. If I'd heard a courting couple moaning in the shadows it might have done the trick, I don't know. But, instead, there was a thin, high squeal like (to show you the direction of my imagination) that made as the lid of a small coffin (of a child being exhumed) is opened on rusty hinges. Only a cat, of course, with a rat by the back of the neck.

Anyhow, here goes! I'm on my way from the warm station buffet, after several glasses of wine, to catch the international express. Passing the brightly-lit bookstall I see, on magazine covers, pale pink nipples set in coppery coronas the size of twopenny pieces.

Here we are, just the one occupant, expanse of crossed thigh, cascade of dark hair out of which a bright eye, after a swift signal, is quickly lowered again.

In actuality the bloody place was so dark that when I climbed into the evil-smelling compartment I wasn't sure if it was the right one. When I did make you out I subsided in the opposite corner.

Silence, deep and dispiriting. How break it? It was you:

'It's not a suitcase left on the seat to keep it for an old lady; it's a sexy young bitch with her skirt up to her waist!'

That completed the débâcle, and whatever insubstantial hope of the slightest chance of deluding myself into the shock of having met, quite by accident, this incredible creature (all female creatures are incredible at a certain pitch of sensual obsession) subtly indicating her readiness to co-operate in my most private fantasies had vanished. A miserable game to have lost, not even having been dicing with the rival lords of cosmos and chaos but with their underlings in a silly charade.

You started to weep (with shame or chagrin?) in the compartment smelling of hopeful, homeward journeys long ago turned sour. Trembling from the chastened aftermath of one of your always excessive moods, you confessed that had it not been for the fear of the armed bands you might encounter you'd have joined the little girls at the quays.

My Herra
And Lazarella,
My delinquent, teenage Mary M.,
My wild and anxious doe,
My bold and timid hare in heat!

When Mullen was making one of his tours of inspection next morning, I spoke to him about the girls with whom I had now more than a nodding relationship since (if from an exaggerated impulse of self-humiliation) you had identified yourself with them.

'We can't ask our homeless lassies up here to share the place with *them*. They're depraved.

'Incidentally,' he went on, 'you might ask Miss Friedlander not to attract all the stray cats in the Laggan to the main hall by feeding them. The place bloody stinks!'

We walked through a couple of renovated rooms in silence and then Mullen said: 'If you've any other suggestions or questions before the official opening now's the time to put them.'

'Just one: Apart from the fact that your armed gangs don't wear uniform, what's the difference between the revolution and the status quo?'

The long sombre line of Mullen's face was broken by a smile.

'Economics, that's what the revolution is about.'

'It's equally about art, sex, religion and nature.'

Perhaps if I was making this report for the politically aware, or, let's say, if I wasn't addressing it primarily to you, I'd get away with such enlightened-seeming statements. But as it is they don't belong where you and I meet. They sound well enough out there on the other side of the desert that surrounds and isolates us in our imaginary city.

You see (*you* do, others are best left in doubt), I care fuck-all for any form of government or administration, for the revolution or the non-revolution or the counter-revolution. I can't believe in, I mean I don't feel, any brotherhood of man that hasn't come about very privately and mostly in small and threatened places.

This morning I felt full of heightened insight, about you, Mullen, myself. Sleeplessness, worry, more-than-usual anxiety (in regard to last night, the business of the sergeant and the sick hare, other vaguer matters, too, related to sex, to growing old, to what you'd 'confessed') made me more responsive not just to what Mullen was saying (the usual stuff) but to signals reaching me from him.

It turned out that he hadn't been either with the Arabs or the Cubans but with a group calling themselves 'The Christian Liberators'.

'They taught me the importance of religious faith as a moral discipline.'

Is there anything that religion *doesn't* mean to somebody or other? No, I didn't ask him, it would have been no good. If you searched among lesser known tribes along the upper reaches of tropical rivers you wouldn't necessarily come on concepts any stranger to you or me than some of Mullen's. And it was only in the utter conviction with which he held them that they differed from the officially-approved ones on this island.

Yet, as I've said, I didn't dislike the man. What I think I mean, though it's hard to be sure when it comes to deeply instinctive likes and dislikes (let alone loves and hates), is that I could have talked him out of any act of violence against me and mine.

Do you know, darling, I used to think I could have done the same with Stalin, but not Hitler, which made me more tolerant of the former monster. I've an idea that Pasternak, in a better position to judge, had a similar feeling.

Mary M. didn't take to social welfare work, far less join the others in promoting the newly-formed Church after the disappearance (that they were already calling the Ascension) of her beloved. She simply, according to you, started singing instead of stripping in the downtown joint (she was nearly out of her teens by then) and a little later there crept into her popular songs a new note.

'After Lazarella's disappearance the songs I liked best were the sad ones too.'

'Such as?'

'*Si tu partais.*'

'Do you regret coming here?' No, not you, I'm back to my talk with Mullen and it's him that's asking.

In our previous talk I'd acted a part as I always do when the conversation turns to polemics (or literature or the weather—not much scope there though for my undoubted gift for charades—) and put on show a deeply thoughtful mind which, though fully conversant with recent revolutionary trends, couldn't unreservedly subscribe to any of them.

'No, I don't.'

(Don't what? Yes, I know I'm telling this rather disconnectedly. Don't regret coming here.)

'And the girl?'

'Why not ask her?'

'I feel awkward with her; she shies away from me; most girls do. Apart from Moira there's not a woman who calls me anything but "Mullen".'

'Was that all he said? About me?'

He said: 'She must have had an unhappy childhood.'

When I wanted to know what made him think that, he said he recognised the signs because he had them himself.

Death had never been a stranger to him, he told me; having often longed for it as a child, he'd come to friendly terms with it. Now when he saw it at close quarters (whether as a result of his own or the enemy's operations) he felt none of the unease he did at the manifestations of sex.

Mullen. I don't know if I entered his secret world for a few moments that morning. I had a glimpse of a burnt-up landscape with the rose gardens of Ismailia still a thirsty dream.

TWENTY-FOUR

Back in our room you were sitting on the unmade bed, a blanket over your drooping shoulders, your face shrouded in hair that looked as if a comb could never again be got through it. It struck me that from watching it so long and anxiously you'd unconsciously fallen into the pose of the hare.

I sat beside you; you turned half away as I put my arms round you. You were naked under the blanket and I felt your nipples swollen under my palms, not in response to my touch but (what was fantasy, what reality?) because of the ecological-neurological union you had with the doe. 'We have not all one body but . . .' If I could recall the rest it might serve as a prayer.

To whom? Christ had evidently washed his hands of us. The Programmer who feeds the cosmic computer with data that it transforms into Magellanic Clouds and the spiral nucleic-acid cell structures couldn't care less. What about the river gods? The Mad Leviathan? Moby Joe? The Sacred Heart? Joby Moe?

Herra, had Noah, who at the time was, as far as I've been able to ascertain, about my present age, given up, as I once mentioned, said 'Shit!' and turned his back to the timbered wall, a sigh-groan-whimper would have gone up from the stalls, pens and hutches that would have been the last-ever ripple of warm breath over the waste of waters. Where thereafter the sightless Whale would ever roam.

'Shall we pray?'

Don't laugh, darling. You hadn't laughed when it might have helped last night in the derelict railway coach, so why laugh now, which, of course, you were a thousand computerised light-years away from doing.

'But don't take your hands away.'

Right! Here goes. I recited what I could recall of the entry in Kafka's Notebooks, dated, but never mind the date: 'We too must suffer all the suffering round us. We have not all one body but we have one way of growing and this leads us through all anguish whether in this form or that. . . . There is no room for justice in this context, but neither is there any room for fear of suffering or for the interpretation of suffering as a merit.'

'Amen,' you said, and although you'd understood hardly anything of what was being talked about (mentally, that is), it worked.

You seemed to straighten up right away, less burdened by all you imagined on top of what you actually experienced.

'Wonderful, wonderful! It's a balance between praying and making love; couples who can't do either should try it. Even those who have no one could find a partner for such a comforting little ceremony.'

That was you and nobody else I ever knew: exhausted in body and spirit one minute, responding a hundred-fold the next.

'Would you mind telling me how to set about it if you're a lonely old man sitting beside the black shell always dumb on the table under the Impressionist print?'

I was remembering the years of isolation when only in fantasy could I find a woman to come back with me and let me put my hands over her breasts while I recited the Kafka piece. 'Oh, I had my instant flights to all parts of the globe, my sex day-dreams, but when I listened all a winter evening for steps on the gravel that I knew well could never come I wasn't what you'd call having a ball.'

With your hair finger-combed behind your ears, you were taking one of your wide, musing glances at me like those with which you seemed to see through the animal mask.

While you were under the shower I looked into the inner part of the hutch. Till my optic nerves adjusted themselves to movements so low down the scale of activity I thought the nest was still. Then, with the same unfamiliar pang as before, I caught the faint up-and-down movement. I parted the veil of the minute temple with my index finger that had never touched or entered a more tender and magic place (not even the female orifice). For a moment before letting the two layers, one of straw, one of fur, fall back, I gazed on the fragile, breathing circle to which I, like you, was linked in the womblike enclosure.

You didn't ask about the leverets when you returned and I didn't mention them, the chances of their surviving being still so slight.

I might wonder how we got through days such as this when now the hour or so between working on this report, or some other task, and the six o'clock aperitif can drag. But I don't; I know that we were either waiting too intensely, you listening and watching, or we were mytholising, entering alternative worlds of my, sometimes of your, imagining. And, above all, there was so much to talk about, whereas these quiet days there are times with nothing to say at all.

We had so much to discuss that we could pick and choose; I didn't tell about that part of my talk with Mullen that I knew wouldn't interest you particularly because it had a political or politico-social theme.

It had started with the character called Des who had driven all over the town unmolested by either side in his big blue van. When I suggested to Mullen that allowing the arms delivery was a high price for the military to pay to persuade the Committee of Five to accept Des as a negotiator between the two factions, he said that the truce was largely phoney and that the military, as distinct from the politicians whose business it was ruining, weren't really concerned to end the fighting.

'They never are as long as hostilities can be kept to an acceptable level. It becomes a way of life to them that they're in no hurry to change.'

'What about you?'

'To some extent its true of us too. People like me aren't fitted anymore, if we ever were, for a peace-time occupation: up on a quiet morning, one ear on the fucking radio weather report, the other waiting to hear how long I have to finish my bloody breakfast . . . just coming up to thirteen-and-a-half-minutes past . . . it's a dry morning but road-works at the junction of . . . and don't forget your car has a heart like yours and give it the protection you wouldn't begrudge yours, would you, commuters, if it worked on a commercial lubricant.'

This is not Mullen verbatim, of course, but the theme is his. What it came to was: he was kept inwardly alive by a closeness to danger and death and the only welcome alternative was in some far, unspecified future when a community such as the station was to be a sketch for might come about.

And don't forget there was sex. I'm talking about *us* again. There's nothing like a sexual ambience, sex in the air, to make time fly.

You jumped up, ran to the window and put out your head.

'Come!'

I followed you down the stairs, two at a time, and out onto the steps of the station where I too caught the distinctive helicopter clatter. But it was growing fainter again and we saw it, a spider climbing the pale, clear wall of sky over the river and disappearing into a crack of distance.

I didn't have to ask you what all the excitement had been about; back in our room I only remarked on the improbability of the sergeant being able to get hold of an army helicopter.

'Why not?'

What you wanted to hear wasn't why not which you knew well enough, but about what could happen in our world within a world.

I wasn't going to humour you, I suppose I didn't really feel like it, but you repeated: 'Tell me why not,' obstinately, on the verge of tears.

'All right. The heavenly armada sails westwards, flanked on the left by a squadron of M.I.G.s and, on the right, by American Phantoms flying in the form of a cross.

'In what looks like a vintage plane comes Chairman Mao sending us a radio message: "May the smallest of the thousand flowers bloom again in the land."'

'Where's the Pope?'

'Oh, he's there too, didn't want to be left out, I dare say, though he does seem a bit out of place. Nor is he at a loss for the right word: "The last and least of the flock shall be saved." And who do you think comes next?'

You shook your head, impatient for me to go on.

'John Clare, restored to sanity after a bout of mental illness by the company of his pet hares, one of which, Puss, lived to the age of eleven and died peacefully one morning in the poet's arms.'

'When was that?'

'A hundred years or so ago.'

'Yes.'

What the murmur meant was that, although not part of your dream of the new world, you saw the justice of associating chosen spirits from the past with this concelebrated act of atonement.

'There's Blake, a bit over-exposed perhaps, but let's give him a welcoming wave, with his tiger and lamb, and, in the old plane from which he parachuted into Crete in World War II, John Lodwick.'

'Eh?'

'My faithful friend and advocate.'

'But what has he to do with it?'

Patience, my love. He tells in one of his novels, dedicated to me and called *Somewhere a Voice is Calling*, about his devotion to a cat that accompanied him on a long train journey through France and Spain in search of a run-away wife or mistress.'

'Did he find her?'

'Found and lost her again, as far as I recall.'

What I didn't tell you was that he also lost the cat from the flat in the Spanish city. Here's the passage which

I read over again one morning in my cubby hole in the loft above the cottage while waiting for your lessons to finish. Lodwick is talking to the girl he lost, found, and was shortly to lose again.

'It may interest you to know,' he said, 'that the cat is dead.'

'No,' said Dominique, horror-stricken.

'Yes, the cat is unfortunately dead. She was killed and skinned about three hours ago.'

'I don't believe you.'

'I'm afraid you are obliged to believe me. I'm afraid we both forgot that there was a branch of a plane tree within five feet of the balcony. Five feet is nothing to a cat. I daresay she thought she could return to us by the same route. She did not know that the neighbourhood was dangerous.'

'Don't talk in that slow way. What are you saying?'

'I am only saying that my cat is dead. I shall have to find somewhere to bury her, too; not that there is much of her to bury, of course.'

But at the time I didn't interrupt my commentary.

'In a winged chariot the Lamb of God has his head dropped on Mary M.'s lap.'

'Sick?'

'Sick as long as our doe is sick. Mary's trip from Tel-Aviv was worse than Lodwick's with his cat. Nobody wanted something escaped from a slaughter house on the plane with them. They had to change at Zürich and she put in the time at the upstairs bar called, I remember, "The Cockpit", drinking wine. It was, incidentally, the same Swiss wine, De Zaley, that the executive had been swilling in the station buffet at not-so-distant Bâle in the other very different story of the night before. It had a sad flavour, not like the heady after-taste of the wine from her family's vineyards at Magdala. (Had she, in her bridesmaid's finery, been handed by Jesus across the table at Cana the glass from which she'd taken her first-ever sip of the fermented juice of the grape?)

'She was the one who had the worst time getting here, though knowing Lodwick, I don't suppose he had a pleasant trip either; he always did things the hard way.'

'Did you know the girl?'

'There were several girls; the one he followed to Spain I only saw a photo of.'

'Was she pretty?'

'For Christsake don't keep interrupting. We haven't yet got to the central figure, the main character in the crowded sky. The sergeant's helicopter is coming towards us where we're waiting just outside the station.'

Liz had been in and out to remind us that you were due for one of your sessions with her but, seeing how absorbed we were, had postponed interrupting. That surprised me, but I think by now she was close to washing her hands of the whole business, would have done so before had it not been for the even more perilous position it would have left her in.

Finally, though, she did claim you, and you, still not fully emerged from the make-believe in which I'd been hiding you, made no more than a token protest.

I went to Liz's room, not to try to write, but to sit and wait. After a bit I couldn't bear it and had to look in next door to catch a glimpse of you.

'I'll make us coffee and when it's ready what about letting her off for to-day?'

Liz smiled at me with the slightly blurred (but it was my eyes that needed glasses, apart from reading) expression that I used to connect with her former hangovers.

As I stood at the stove in the kitchen it was as if I'd accidentally stepped onto a moving platform. Things started shifting in relation to me until I was back at the cottage at an indeterminate point of time. Pain was in the air but it had to coalesce into a visual form before I could recall the details.

Who was it carrying in her arms the body of the cat that had sighed out a last breath early that morning as we had kept vigil, you or Nancy? Who had borne it in her arms towards the garden as she'd done so often when we had strolled there on a summer morning, but, realising that this morning I was waiting a little impatiently by the grave I'd been digging, turned back? Ah, that change of direction, so slight, a whole end-of-the-world was in it!

Was it long before I'd met you that I watched that heart-breaking turn at the garden gate? Pain evokes the same gestures in diverse bodies, even, and it was you called my attention to this, simulating in animals attitudes of human despair.

When I'd seen the hunched-up doe with head dropped sideways I'd thought (but, I'm sure, a few seconds after you) of pictures of Jesus on the cross with his chin against his chest.

Put the lesson books aside, comb your hair behind your ears, or while you lift it from the back of your neck like a sheaf let Liz slip the ribbon under it and bring the ends round to tie in a loose bow on top. Let's see your face as you sip the coffee.

Your hope was set on the weed that the sergeant had promised to find, and you asked me whether in all my experience as a gardener at the cottage (the cottage was in the air again) I'd an idea of what wild herb it might be.

Could I only think of something, have at least a small part in the possible cure! I could recall many different kinds of weeds, especially their roots which were what I'd had to deal with, but nothing came to mind to indicate special qualities in any of them.

'I'd better go and do the shopping while it's quiet.'

I knew, and so did you, that Liz was waiting for one of us to accompany her to the row of shops whose lights were always on behind boarded-up windows that was the ghetto shopping-centre, but to-day you didn't look up or open your mouth.

When she had gone you heaved a sigh and lay your cheek on the table. I slipped my hand between it and the wood and thus began the second phase in a long, memorable day.

'Aren't you going to work this morning?'

I shook my head, a gesture you couldn't see because your face was turned sideways on a level with the table-top, but you well knew there was no question of my gathering together the scattered fragments of the trance in which to write.

'Then tell me about the desert city.'

Make-believes, fairy-tales, legends: they were your alternative reality as fiction was mine.

'It's hard to get back there from where we are now.'

'Suppose there's a last train standing here in this station that's going there. We are sitting in it waiting, waiting, not really believing it will start. We've been talking and eating sandwiches and drinking beer all day and towards evening we glance out and the platform seems to be moving. We're silent, we daren't say a word, we just hold our breath; it'll stop again in a moment, it's being shifted a few yards up the platform so the goods wagon is handier for loading. But it goes quicker, we're really on our way!'

No good asking: Where, my love?

'I think what first made me long for the desert city was reading an account of the opening of the Suez Canal. The town of Ismailia, half-way along it, had been partially rebuilt and laid out for the occasion. The streets had a gala air that evening and from the little square the first ships, beflagged and lit-up, could be seen sailing into the lake from either end.'

'Who were there?'

'The Empress of Austria was strolling in the garden of one of the villas among the roses and fountains where a short time before the desert had stretched.'

'With you?'

'Perhaps, though she wouldn't have been my cup of tea.'

'What did you talk about?'

'Let's see. She asked my opinion of Joyce.'

'Who's that?'

No, you'd never heard of him. Wonderful! Without going as far as saying I couldn't love a girl who'd heard of Joyce (I'd had my fill of him from Nancy), let's say I'd have been too bloody self-conscious with one who knew *Ulysses* backwards to . . .

'After strolling in the rose garden, what then? Didn't you go up to the royal apartment in the villa?'

I'd have gone fucking anywhere if I'd thought I could keep your attention and distract you a bit longer. But this morning my city wasn't either deep enough in its desert nor sufficiently aglow with its own fantastic light to shut us into itself.

You were back from where I'd tried to rescue you temporally.

'My heart's hare.'

Your heart's hare; but your hare's heart was cold from the age-old fear that had infiltrated your human blood.

Liz returned with news of an increase of the number of guerrillas out in the streets and at the barricades. She had also brought a hand-printed leaflet announcing a public gathering at the station for that afternoon.

None of this news was welcome.

'George won't get through,' was your first thought, and your second, before I'd had time to reply: 'I'll go to the barracks and wait for him there.'

'You'd be spotted, if not actually followed. I'd have a better chance myself if I rang the barracks and left a message for him to meet me in the town.'

'Don't leave me.'

There were a dozen ways in which the plan could misfire and if I ended up in the custody of either camp what was going to happen to you, not to mention Liz?

The mood of your god of chance, once discernible, doesn't change quickly. The doe was, that was my superstitious fear, affected by the first ripples from a new tide of adversity about to flow over us; of course I didn't share these gloomy insights, if that is what they were, with you.

In the early afternoon one of Mullen's bodyguards, who we'd seen firing his sub-machinegun at the helicopter, brought a message telling me, rather belatedly, about the meeting at four o'clock.

TWENTY-FIVE

The old waiting room, with the newly-made bunks stacked along a wall and the slogans we had posted up looking out-of-place, was crowded. The rows of seats, salvage from a burnt-out concert hall, were almost full.

Shrinking from a place in the vanguard of this invasion, I was going to take a back seat but Mullen caught sight of me from the platform and conducted me onto it. There were three others already there; I don't suppose their identities matter much now, except that of the only other member of the Committee we were to meet and whose Christian name was all I ever was told and, even then, on different occasions, as Frank and Arthur.

We were seated at a table on which an old rain coat covered a bulky shape. In my innocence I imagined an unveiling ceremony. Had a piece of sculpture, or a historic memento of an earlier siege of the town, that time the whole of it, been donated and was about to be placed by Mullen and his lieutenants on one of the badly-cracked plinths at the entrance from which the former statues had been blasted?

A short speech by Mullen announcing that the semi-truce unofficially agreed on and partially observed between the guerrillas and the security forces was at an end.

'That bastard who's been driving all over the place in his van on the strength of conducting negotiations informed me last night that his fat slob of a father had flatly refused our final terms,' Mullen whispered as he sat down to a bleak silence.

'His father?'

'O.C., the paras.'

The young man wearing a beret and dark glasses had got to his feet and was talking about trajectories and velocities. For a moment I thought the meeting was some sort of half-disguised training session which, though, was hardly compatible with the presence of journalists, who were easily recognisable, to say nothing of the middle-aged and elderly women.

The guerrilla officer was accusing the security forces of unnecessarily using cartridges of a velocity of several thousand foot seconds (I took notes; you'd made me promise you a detailed account) because of their terrible shock effect. Worse, they were firing hollow-point bullets, commonly called dum-dum, whose special attributes were now going to be demonstrated.

From somewhere (under the raincoat? If so, without disturbing the main object concealed) a square of semi-transparent material appeared on the table. There was an uneasy stir along the rows as the whispered word 'gelignite' was passed along, but the young man smiled and assured us that no explosive substance was involved.

'I am going to fire a solid bullet into the gelatine which reacts sufficiently like human or animal tissue to give you an idea of the difference in the wounds caused.'

He stepped to the end of the platform with a Luger pistol in his hand.

How do I know what weapon it was? Our relationship

was too short and too intensely taken up with day-to-day developments for there to have been time—no long winter evenings by the fire—for me to tell you of even the principal involvements of a long and active lifetime. One had been in a civil war you hadn't as much as heard of, from when I'd kept contacts with certain armed groups in the other part of the island.

The first shot penetrated the block of gelatine without distorting it. The guerrilla then reloaded the gun with what he explained was a Hornet bullet similar to the type being used in the rifles of enemy snipers.

What's all this? I hear you ask. Surely nobody expects what's happening here, and in all the other parts of the world, to be done humanely and with pity?

As the second shot entered the gelatine it was convulsed on the table, one side ballooning into a huge swelling with protuberances and prolapses all over the writhing, shapeless mass.

This, then, was the curtain-raiser to the main spectacle.

'I'm trying to guess what that was.'

Nobody better fitted imaginatively to do so; your nightmares revealed as facts was nothing new.

When the curtain did rise it was on a peaceful enough scene (at first glance): a brown-and-white, mongrel bitch (swollen tits showed she had lately pupped) apparently asleep on the table-stage. At a second scrutiny it was mercifully evident she was already, if not long, dead.

'I don't think I want to hear more of this.'

Fold the half sheet of paper on which I'd made my notes and change the subject. You were, as I suppose you'd been most of that afternoon, at our ordinary, familiar table—no hint of mortuary slab or altar top—

chin in palms, face half-hidden in a straggle of lack-lustre locks.

'Did it ooze blood?'

'I don't think so; but it did everything short of bleed at the second shot.'

'What?'

A sick curiosity? Depends on what you call 'sick'. Rather, an idea, mistaken or not, never to flinch from 'facts'.

'It turned in a series of jerks into a grotesque monster of indeterminate proportions that quivered for perhaps twenty seconds after the blast.'

'Nature flows in jerks,' you murmured, 'blossoms open in little jerks, with a day or more between each, as I once saw in a speeded-up film, we make love in jerks, and now it seems we're destroyed like that too.'

You were watching the doe hunched in the corner from which she hadn't moved, through a chink in the strands of hair, and listening for a step on the stairs, though it was still too early. Your wrists were covered in the long-sleeved jersey you'd changed into.

After the waiting room had emptied Mullen had locked the door and given me the key that I had hung on a nail on our landing to be collected by the workmen when they arrived in the morning.

'How was it?'

It was you asking about the meeting: there was no point my enquiring about the doe.

'All right. Shall I make us a cup of tea?'

It was all I could think of: isn't it the last small gesture we'll make (not you and I, those left, I mean) as, in our small craft, we sight Joby Moe, more solemnly known as the Abomination of Desolation, rushing down on us with the blind fury of the exploding sun?

When I'd laid the patterned tray with the two blue cups and the big, brown pot (with exaggerated care and orderliness) and placed it on the table by our bed, you gave me your missal that you'd opened at the passage where Christ raises Lazarus and asked me to read it out.

Who was it had once made the same request? Raskolnikov to Sonia in *Crime and Punishment*? A book you certainly hadn't read. While waiting for the tea to draw (what quiet moments does the phrase recall!), I made a start: 'Now a certain man was sick, named Lazarus, of Bethany, the town of Mary and her sister Martha. It was that Mary which anointed the Lord with ointment, and wiped his feet with her hair, whose brother Lazarus was sick. Therefore his sisters sent unto him, saying, Lord, behold, he whom thou lovest is sick. When Jesus heard that, he said, this sickness is not unto death. . . .

'Now Jesus loved Martha, and her sister, and Lazarus. When he had heard therefore that he was sick, he abode two days, still in the same place where he was.'

I broke off to pour the tea and after we'd each taken a ceremonious sip you asked the old, old question (though new to you) as to why Christ wasted two days before hurrying to his dying friend.

'The official interpretation is that Lazarus had to die so that Christ could perform the famous miracle.'

'That's how the official interpreters would have acted had they been Christ, with cold-blooded calculation. Did it never strike you that he might have known of a concoction of wild herbs to cure his friend and was looking everywhere for them?'

'No. Nor would it have occurred to you in other circumstances.'

'So what?'

'He saith unto them, our friend Lazarus sleepeth; but I go so that I may wake him out of sleep. Then said his disciples, Lord, if he sleeps he shall do well. Howbeit Jesus spake of his death. . . . Then Jesus said to them plainly, Lazarus is dead. . . . Then when Jesus came he found that he had lain in the grave four days already. . . . Then Martha as soon as she heard that Jesus was coming, went and met him, but Mary sat still in the house. . . . Jesus said unto her, I am the resurrection and the life. . . . Believest thou this? She saith unto him, Yea, Lord. . . .

'And when she had so said, she went her way and called Mary her sister secretly, saying, The Master is come, and calleth for thee. As soon as she heard that, she arose quickly, and came unto him. . . . The Jews then that were with her in the house, and comforted her, when they saw Mary, that she rose up hastily and went out, followed her, saying, She goeth unto the grave to weep there.'

'What a lot she had to weep over: Jesus' feet, graves and the cross. And the other smaller things, not recorded, like her own unbearable thoughts.'

'I suppose so.'

You were getting worked up by this ancient tale into making yourself believe that the sergeant would come with his medicinal weed and cure the doe. First, he had to find it, then get into the barricaded area before the creature expired and, even after that, the cure had still to work.

'Go on.'

I didn't like your feverish impatience to hear the final dramatic words.

'Mary was patient, waiting in her room.'

'She hadn't already lost a loved creature that never returned.'

I left out several sentences, anxious to come to the end of the story that you were so desperately clinging to: 'And when he had thus spoken, he cried with a loud voice, Lazarus, come forth. . . . And he that was dead came forth.'

'She must have overflowed with gratitude, and what give in return?'

Should I be brought to the Grand Aula on some last-day, end-of-term examination and asked to state before the three examiners (one at least a woman) on what, if any, aspect of reality I wished to answer questions, there would be only one on which to base a claim of a not totally wasted lifetime. I would say, with a certain quiet confidence: Set me a paper on waiting.

I have no doubt such an examination paper exists among the huge number kept to test every candidate. Each must be questioned only in his or her own, however narrow or curious, field, and even those who it turns out have had little contact with reality of any sort may, for all I know, have tests that could exonerate them.

I have waited in all kinds of places including (though that part of my life I'd no time to tell you much about) a number of prison cells. I learnt how the living consciousness is slowly walled up inside the minutes, hours, days and weeks, how, inside the windowless, soundproof cell constructed of future time, the mind wakes each morning to be invaded by brute actuality into its lingering dream and yet still survives to imagine and hope.

Comrade Examiners, I claim a knowledge of waiting second to none but those of old whose classic example Herra drew my attention to that day in our room in the station when she asked me to read out the account of the raising of Lazarus from the dead. And of course to the girl herself (take second place, I mean) if only because of her long and hopeless wait for Lazarella.

If, as I understand, life is for learning one of the vast number of subjects taught here (almost all of them painful), let me be examined on the subject of waiting.

'What kind of questions do you expect?'

'The ones that only someone who knew the subject inside out would think of asking, like your Mary M.'

TWENTY-SIX

After the hare had crawled into the inner compartment (to die?) and remained there for what seemed several hours there was a step on the stairs.

You didn't jump up to open the door as you would have even a couple of days earlier; hopes destroyed and fruitless waiting in the past had caught up with, and chastened, you. It was I who called 'come in' in answer to the knock. Only when the door opened and you saw the waiting was over did you let out the half-word, half-sigh: 'George!'

'Yes, it's yours truly.'

A touch of the facetious to cover some initial awkwardness, but, at the same time, a quick glance round the room for the hare that he didn't see.

'Don't tell me I'm too late?'

'She's in there,' you pointed, 'has been for hours.'

He took from the jacket pocket of the grey flannel suit (which would have distinguished him as an alien as much as his accent had he been spotted in the dark and questioned) a few feathery leaves and laid them on the table. You regarded them with the awed, musing glance I'd seen you turn on certain of your magic talismans such as the watch and cuff-links in the water garden.

To me it looked an undistinguished weed; had I seen it growing on the garden bank at the cottage between the dandelions and cow-parsley I don't suppose I'd have given it a second look.

'Like me to try her with it?'

You nodded, not voicing your fear that the doe was dead.

He knelt down by the hutch and opened the door to the inner compartment; because his back was in the way neither of us could see in. Another wait, short by the clock but long enough for the sergeant to have examined a prostrate body and assured himself it was lifeless before giving us the news, or, alternatively, to have made several attempts and failed to get the doe to nibble the proffered weed.

As I was about to break the silence with a whispered question, he closed the door and got to his feet, turned and gave us a nod.

A nod, though it hadn't struck me before, can mean anything from: 'Yes, it looks like the end (of a journey, a life, the world)', to: 'Why, of course, it's my old friend, Arthur.' What this portended I wasn't, nor, I knew, were you, at all sure.

'We'll leave her alone with the stuff for a bit.'

More waiting but, to those who've learnt to distinguish the different kinds and degrees, we were a little further back, there was slightly more shelter between us and the exposed edge with its view of the void.

'How did you manage to get here?' I asked.

'In a van.'

'A blue one?'

'A laundry van, sir.'

How did his calling me 'sir' place me? As an elder

brother of your father's? An evidently serious-minded, if eccentric, old fellow whose presence here was another of the mysteries that active service in these conditions was full of?

'What about getting out again?'

'You're not in a hurry, are you, George?'

Your hope was in him and his continued presence.

'The van will pick me up when the laundry has been delivered.'

The laundry, it seemed, had been opened to help lessen unemployment in the no-go areas and had customers on both sides of the barricades. That it might serve another purpose to the security forces crossed my mind.

The sergeant had brought you a present, though anything he could have brought became insignificant beside the feathery leaves on their long, pale stalks.

'It's a bit the worse for wear, Herra; been in the house since I was a boy.'

Which was how it looked: a tattered volume with the cover half off, once a children's favourite and then tucked away on a kitchen shelf.

'I'll keep it safe and give it back next time you come.'

You'd no idea what the book was about. It was a link with the sergeant and he was a link with hope.

You glanced at a couple of dog-eared pages and started to read out, partly, I suppose, to bridge one of the recurring silences.

'I once shot one running from hounds. Well, when I opened that hare I was never so much surprised. There wasn't a mite of blood in it. That blood was all gone in pink bubbles. . . . It had run the life out of itself. They'd been hunting that thing for nearly half-an-hour.'

'Keep it,' the sergeant told you.

Silence. Liz joins us. She still doesn't know who the sergeant is or where he's from. I've slipped into the present tense without meaning to because when I relive the events in this report I am still there in the upper room that evening, when for the last (and almost the first) time all who have a place in the story (except those like Lodwick, Nancy and Lazarella whose place is dependent on either your or my memory at any given moment) are gathered there.

'Hark!'

Don't say the sergeant had heard the sound of the van come to pick him up!

No; for a moment later it reached my consciousness too from wherever it had first vibrated: a wild, muted cry, echo of the ripples of a tide returning.

A moment in history, my history, dividing one era from the next.

A shadow squeezed itself through the opening in the dividing wall of the hutch, took shape in the outer compartment, and appeared before us, bobbing across the room, not to the corner that may have smelt of sickness and death but to another where it sat with ears erect.

'There you are!'

Yes, indeed, or: 'Glory be!'

The sergeant's slightly bemused expression (which you once told me he only wore when I was present) changed briefly as he looked at you. But you didn't seem to catch his glance (how wrong I was) and, after Liz had gone to prepare the evening meal (though I was wrong about that too), sat on the edge of our bed, leaning back against the cushions that served us as pillows at night.

The position caught up your mini-skirt, exposing your thighs right to where I saw the pale shimmer between them of the knickers under your tights.

I can analyse what happened then till the heifers come lowing home; I can catch subconscious signals between you and the sergeant till the air is crackling with them to explain to myself your taking the sergeant by the hand and having him follow you out of the room. But the veteran in me, trained in the hard discipline of the defence of interior ghettos stepped out onto the landing, exposing myself to the enemy in the shape of the nail that should have had the waiting-room key hanging on it. And hadn't.

I stood stock still, the old animal instinct to dissolve into the background at moments of danger, in this case wood and linoleum, but was hauled back into full view by Liz calling from her room.

She was standing just inside her door with a folded sheet in her hand.

'If there's anything not clear please ask me.'

Just the moment to serve me with her notice; oh, yes, I guessed what it was.

'You're not happy here, Liz?'

She shook her head impatiently, to indicate this wasn't the real question at all.

'But what will you do for God's sake?'

What will *I* do was more like it now that my love has left me? But, of course, I knew you hadn't, even if I didn't quite understand your not treating sex as solemnly as most of those of my generation did.

'You haven't read all.'

'What?'

For a moment I'd forgotten everything, including the

letter, but you and the sergeant on one of the newly-constructed bunks.

'I said why don't you read the rest.'

'I can't with you standing there (seemingly rereading what she'd typed on my machine, over my shoulder). For Christsake let's sit down.'

'All right.'

'God, what's this?'

'What's wrong with you, Sugrue; you're as nervy as a kitten?'

It seemed she'd been a student at the university when I was lecturing there a couple of terms. No, I couldn't recall her among the thirty or forty in my class.

'Did you never come up and put one of those irrelevant questions they were always asking after one of my talks?'

'I was far too shy.'

Those old lectures had found a response in at least one youthful imagination. She had even copied down what she recalled of the poems of mine I used to read to them when I ran out of literary talk.

One of them, dated from the war and, like the others, never published, began:

'September deepens and the nights are long
And through that fearful autumn damp with blood
There shines the other autumn of his song . . .'

'That was *my* wonderful autumn,' the letter went on, 'when I used to go back to my room to tend the rose garden that you and Keats had planted in my heart.'

Later she had got a teaching job that had some, if not much, connection with literature but even less with her notions of rose gardens. Then, still young, she had married and entered a rose garden of her very own where, however, some very nasty weeds soon got the better of her at first devoted, and then despairing, weeding. After leaving her husband she'd gone abroad and had taught in several schools increasingly threatened by the discovery of all the nights she spent in her substitute, alcohol-induced rose garden, before the Swiss one where you and she met.

'If the three of us lived in the sort of world that you and I were brought up in, Liz, and that still exists in minds well-sheltered behind various institution walls, then your conviction that you're drawing your monthly salary from Mrs. Friedlander on false pretences would have some justification.'

Doesn't that deserve a 'Bravo'? Imagine the discipline and detachment required to come out with so reasoned and felicitously expressed an argument when the moment before and the moment after I'd seen you spreadeagled under the sergeant on the very table where the previous morning (was it?) the other exhibition had been staged!

She was suddenly very dejected, as I saw when I glanced at her before skimming through the penultimate paragraph. I'm not sure what she'd expected, but neither her giving notice nor the news of her adolescent infatuation were going to carry us away into a simultaneous emotional crisis.

In the one-but-last paragraph she thanked me for restoring her confidence in herself and thus helping her from becoming an irredeemable wino, as she put it. That gave me a pang even then when I was pretty well insulated under layers of pangs of my own.

In the last sentence she blamed a morning hangover for her carelessness in not spotting your absence from the group till too late and thus being responsible for your abduction and subsequent incarceration in this God-forsaken place, as she called it, to which your mother had been forced into giving her consent.

Her principles: they were what she had hoped she was standing up for, if belatedly. But when I didn't as much as mention the sacrifice she was making for their sake, things became darker and more complicated than she'd thought they ever could again.

How do I know? We talked about it by the stove one winter evening when these events were part of the legendary past.

TWENTY-SEVEN

You had slipped back, had a shower, changed into jeans and were standing in the doorway of Liz's room.

'Here I am, as good as new!'

A cold shock of a remark that revealed, as no amount of argument would, the difference in our attitudes to sex. It took my breath away and momentarily I couldn't open my mouth.

'No grudges?'

I shook my head. No, no, no! But I was sick with the old jealousies.

'O.K.?' you persisted.

'More than that, it's wonderful.'

'Isn't it, Liz?' you asked her.

'I hadn't time to tell her yet.'

You were astonished; you'd been sure that that was why I was here.

'Tell me what?' Poor Liz, she was even more confused.

'Our hare, the apple of our eye, is cured.'

I don't know how, but she managed a smile out of her misery; perhaps it was just a thoughtless reflection from your face and burnished hair.

'Where's George?'

If Liz could smile so bravely, I could ask and give him his name.

'The van picked him up.'

How many questions remained unresolved! Liz hadn't withdrawn her notice and, you told me later, had sent off applications for other jobs. Had you another date with the sergeant, and did it involve an implicit promise? Was my failure to make love to you the other night caused solely by anxiety over the hare? Or was my Aaron's Rod losing its magic power of joining me to you?

Problems, doubts, uncertainties. . . . We'd never had them before. But your joy at the saving of the life of one small creature in the middle of so much savagery of all sorts, not to mention its tender brood, helped me keep my gloomier thoughts at the fringe of my mind.

On the second night after the doe's semi-resurrection you, with unimaginable sweetness, dispelled my gathering neurosis.

We were in bed and I hadn't taken you in my arms for fear of not being able to drift away with you on the unproblematic, relaxed sensual tide, gently tossed in the undulations of its mid-ocean waves.

'Shall I tap on his shell and call out three times: Old snail, come forth!'

You'd hardly got the silly words out of your mouth than I knew they'd have the effect that all my serious self-probings were prohibiting. When I felt the touch of your cool, cool finger in mock enquiry as to what, for Christsake, was the delay, we were half-way there. Where? Half-way down the hill and picking up speed. Say it; put it into a plain, simple sentence and no poetics! Whisper in my ear.

But before I'd time to string together the, mostly, four-letter evocations of the act and organs involved, you said: 'About the other business . . .'

'What business?' But heart, as well as the lower organ, had leapt.

'If George turns up again, as he said he'd try to if only to find good homes for the leverets, I made it plain that . . .' I put my hand over your mouth.

In the morning word came from Mullen fixing the day for the official opening of the station.

There had been signs of what I now saw as last-minute preparations, and scraps of news had reached us via Liz who picked them up in the rumour-relaying interiors of dark little shops with boarded-up windows. Wary though I am both by nature and because of what I've had in the way of dealings with authority of various kinds, I was feeling too relieved (and relief is for me the most tangible part of happiness) to wonder why I hadn't been told till the last minute.

A group of volunteers were at work early setting up a trestle table in the main hall.

'Who have been invited?' I asked Mullen.

'To the cold repast? Just a few locals and some visitors from outside. There'll be the general gathering afterwards with a few remarks from some of us.'

'Remarks?'

'They'll want to know what it's all in aid of.'

I too. Not that I came out with this, realising in time that he expected some of the 'remarks' to be mine.

There were things about myself that I'd only become clear about lately. My imaginative insights, such as they were (that's to say, erratic), and my alternative worlds, were concerned with the very private, not the public, sector. I was a minus sign in the social revolutionary heavens, in spite of the few readers who became immersed in my fiction feeling they were being shown down narrow alleys where the well-dressed and law-abiding never ventured.

Mullen had quickly passed on to a more agreeable aspect of the ceremony (I supposed the thought of my 'remarks' weighed on him, for a different reason as much as on me): the menu.

'Salmon and crayfish, caught from our doorstep you might say, in the estuary.'

At twelve-thirty by the century-old station clock (as the watch-maker to whom we'd given it for overhaul had pronounced it) now back on the newly-whitewashed wall above the booking-office in which the cold lunch was ready to be served through the guichets (did these imaginative little touches really come from Mullen or was it possible you'd been secretly consulted?) a company of leather-jacketed, black-bereted youths marched onto the arrival platform.

They were followed by those with admission cards among the crowd gathered in the rubble-filled square.

At least I could draw Mullen's attention to the bookstall that we'd stocked for the occasion with whatever we could get hold of: a novel of mine that I'd noticed in Peter's cabin and borrowed, your wild life books, some volumes of poetry and a few long out-of-date periodicals of the literary Left in French. But Mullen wasn't attending; he'd just heard what he'd been listening for. You touched my arm to stop me talking rubbish and listen too, for not only had you been in the secret, you'd had a hand in its arranging.

The sounds I heard and the sight I saw was not far short of the imaginary one I'd described to you while waiting for the sergeant. A passenger train drawn by an ancient locomotive was, with a shrill escape of steam that brought back excitements of long ago, entering the station.

A moment on the grand historic scale, equalling the arrival of the first sea-going vessel into the lake at Ismailia.

Moving, totally unexpected (you and Mullen and the railway officials had been planning it for weeks without me guessing anything) and, as I was to feel in a moment, personally touching.

You'd even thought of going south and travelling back in the carriage from the southern capital that had, after several shuntings, been joined to the rest of the train at its point of departure three or four stations down the line. Only the hare's sickness had stopped you at the last moment.

It was from this carriage at the rear of the train, thus they were among the last to reach us, that the three poets, whom you'd planned to appeal to personally to come, came into sight.

Embracings from you, enarmings with me, handshakes for Mullen. Hayden, Bill and John, whom you'd met but once before, you were at once at home with as you'd never been, apart from me, with any human.

When all had studied the hand-decorated menu and fetched their chosen food from the guichets, the wine (like the menu, another thoughtful touch of yours) and beer poured, there was time to take a look at the company.

'Did Mullen say a cleric was going to pronounce the place open for others besides the stray cats that have been benefiting from it for quite a time?'

'Somebody dressed as a priest more likely; doesn't look right to me.'

His not 'looking right' could have been due to my being without my long-distance glasses which I'd discarded since selling the Rolls, not that even the earlier part of the proceedings weren't soon blurred, as I tried to recall them, through intoxication's retrospective effect.

A dangerous sense of relaxation, of taking my rightful place at last in the best of all possible worlds, that's what I was conscious of, standing between you and your governess, our plates reassuringly piled with pale pink fruit from this northern estuary and our glasses filled (to me a matter of even greater satisfaction) with the dark elixir. Each gulp I took further confirmed my impression that our situation was extremely satisfactory and the future even brighter. As for the problems that had been worrying me, I had trouble in even recalling them; yes, there was Liz's letter, but that, and any others, would probably dissolve away on their own. If not, I could easily deal with them.

This sense of all being well, an assurance that I normally lack completely, as do you, was, of course, a presage of disaster. For your sake I'd better explain that these drug-induced states mostly end in behaviour that makes me groan to recall later.

'Could I have some prawns, please?'

'There aren't any, darling.'

'Whatever it was, then.'

'What was?'

I had trouble grasping that you were asking for another helping of crayfish, but as soon as I did it was wonderful to be able to make up for the misunderstanding by taking your plate to the guichet to have it replenished. As I stood waiting for it to be handed back my heart was as artificially light as when strolling with the imaginary empress in the rose garden.

Rotten drunk, that's what I was by now, sailing gaily without navigation lights, chart or compass.

In the belief that the tide of fortune (or misfortune) once set in does not suddenly ebb, I was expecting some piece of good news. In such a state even neutral news can be turned to wonderful advantage.

It might even come from Mullen who had begun to speak from the other end of the table or from the coloured girl quite close with a smile like a small white flag hoisted to hail me.

'This new man begins his life like a man at the end of it; he considers himself as a potential corpse. He will be killed; not only does he accept the risk, he is sure of it . . . he has seen so many dying men that he prefers victory to survival; others, not he, will have the fruit of victory; he is too weary of it all. But this weariness of heart is the root of an unbelievable courage. We find our humanity on this side of death and despair; he finds it beyond torture and death.'

Inspiring stuff, all right, but not quite the news I was waiting for. Unless, that is, I identified myself with this grim revolutionary figure from Sartre (that's who Mullen had quoted), but even with my capacity to enter briefly into various roles, this didn't seem to fit my mood.

Refill my own and the coloured girl's glass, reaching over to do so into the dusky, moonlit middle distance, then wait for the general relaxation of attitudes of attentiveness at the end of Mullen's speech (it had become tedious now that I saw it wasn't going to touch me on the expectant nerve) and see the direction of the warm rain clouds.

They gathered themselves together and approached, nodding, as I interpreted their graceful undulation, in the direction of the deserted platform. I would have liked to bring my glass with me in case I needed to add to the buoyancy that was carrying me along and I began to lose height and momentum.

Which is what apparently happened, because one of the next recollections is her asking: 'Man, are you high, because if you are you surely know you're wasting both our times, and I don't often get the chance of such a good one, by bringing me in here?'

In where? Looked like the former station-master's office.

I'd imagined diverting this big river flowing, moonlit, through the heart of the dark continent so that it flowed through me. Or I flowed into it.

As I wandered disconsolately along the platform, turned out of my mythical Africa, I was met and accompanied back to the party by the three poets so that my reappearance could have been from a stroll with them and not a miserable retreat.

My wine glass was where I had left it and so were you. Yes, Herra, that's the order in which I took stock of the situation.

It is by telling you these shameful things, made doubly so by the point in time when they occurred, that guilt doesn't poison my memories.

The priest was making the official opening speech and I caught parts of it from far away. Distances were extending, the universe in my immediate neighbourhood was expanding and, relatively, objects like my wine glass were getting smaller, which meant having to refill it more often.

'You've established a haven where nothing is bought or sold in the midst of our universal consumer-and-consumed society. Christ chased the money changers from the temple, and you've replaced the advertisements calling for more and more spending in an ever madder search for the promised beatitude of Value-for-Money with slogans of your own.

'These posters of yours have nothing to sell, no useful commodities or services to offer. In fact they're blessedly out of place in a utilitarian culture.

'You are our social philosophers and one of you, I hear, is an artist. Non-utilitarians. Heidegger asked: "What use is philosophy? What is it useful for? It is no use at all. It is useful for nothing." We can repeat those words as an antidote to the other litany echoing everywhere outside: "Use this, get better value there, economise with A, B goes further, C lasts longer, D pays for itself twice over."

'When all these products are bought, used and consumed on the way to the promised land, what is it like when we get there, what is the End Product, the final achievement? Pollution!'

'Doesn't sound like a cleric, he's here on false pretences.'

'In declaring this Hall of Freedom open, may I congratulate all those concerned in its conception? And let me also felicitate the two of you who have special cause for rejoicing.'

There you are! Who but the sergeant could have told him of the hare's recovery?'

'For Christsake! He means you and Mullen, not you and me.'

But it added to the fun-fair for me to unmask an agent of the security forces.

'Imagine a priest commenting favourably on the posters!'

TWENTY-EIGHT

The hum of talk died down; who were they waiting for now?

'You.' Your whisper was loud enough for most of the company to overhear.

Take a last swig from my glass, pass my hand over my brow in a gesture that, while giving me a moment in which to recollect myself, might help nip the giggling in the bud.

Before getting out a word I had to cope with a rush of thoughts returning from such far-flung areas as the humid valleys of Zambesi and Limpopo, the gardens (long vanished) of Ismailia, as well as, nearer at hand, the sergeant's mess where I'd just been imagining George regaling one of the dusty-footed nymphs from the waterside.

What I needed was a well-defined subject to start me off on the right note. Where find one amid the inner confusion? Suddenly I recalled this pale, slim, wooden object on a polished table. What on earth was it, and from where had this recollection come? But anything was enough to start me off.

'I'm not going into all kinds of social, political and kindred matters. Let me tell you very simply how I see our Hall of Peace and Freedom: like a room in a side-street of a city at night from whose open window comes the sound of a flute.' (That's what I'd remembered noticing in your room at your mother's during my visit there and had never thought about since.)

'Any of you who have been hurrying to or from some harassing appointment, or place of so-called entertainment, and have paused to listen, will know what I mean.'

How was that, darling? I paused and looked at you.

'I stopped playing it when I started to like sadder tunes.'

Was that before or after we'd met at your mother's? But if I'd asked you the prolonged interruption in my talk might have restarted the sniggers.

'I won't elaborate except to say that we have three poets here with us, which I take as a good omen. Poetry is the chief of the utterly useless commodities that, as the last speaker put it, we can oppose to the universal faith in the God of Value, whose earthly manifestation is Christ, Computer.'

Yes, I was off again on a slightly different tack, one that would allow me to indulge in another of my passions. Which one? My one-man sortie against the company of writers who form a well-trained body-guard to prevent any surprise assault on, or disturbance of, our culture.

'On this island we have a host of writers, good, bad and mediocre. The few good ones and the large number of bad ones have their uselessness to a utilitarian, consumer society in common. It's the middle lot, the medium number, who compromise with this society by writing commentaries on it, creating people who fit its ideas of what fictional characters should be: close relatives of those in works already safely established as literature.'

Did I grudge their renown? If my own novels were

alluded to at all it was in some such phrase as that they 'add a piquant flavour to our cultural heritage' (an outlandish sauce poured over the local dish for which we are justly famed, especially across the Atlantic).

I was about to name two or three of the best-known and most highly-respected of my *bêtes noirs* when I saw the three poets regarding me. Once again they had rescued me from my dangerous and, in this case, gratuitous, obsessions.

I ended instead by mentioning another of the random memories that I kept recalling. It was a favourite song of my childhood and the opening verse had evoked the magic havens that even then I had dreamed of, beginning with the ark and now ending with the opening of the converted station.

> 'Roses are blooming in Picardy
> In the hush of the silver dew.'

Of course it was beyond me to communicate to any of the by-now restless audience, except the three poets and, possibly, the priest, why the song, with its rather tawdry words, appealed to me. Picardy, like, say, Ismailia, meant nothing to them, they wouldn't even know it as the part of northern France where the fiercest battles of the First World War had been fought. There was no mention of the war in the song, either because it had been composed earlier or because the song-writer's intention was to celebrate the return of peace to a ravaged corner of the earth. In either case it evoked for me a flat, undistinguished countryside still bearing its terrible scars and, because of them, with small, lovingly-tended gardens on the outskirts of market towns, in one of which, as I passed on the still, warm evening of the song, a woman was watering the roses. As, too, which I had started by trying to tell them, I'd heard the notes of the flute (that you'd given up playing before I met you) from an open window at night in a city.

No, nobody but you and the poets knew that I was telling them about the function of the converted station.

The latter part of the afternoon is lost in mists of intoxication. Waking when it was already dark in our room, I groaned at what I recollected and feared there might be even more discreditable episodes that I didn't. I reached out a hand into the pool of pure silence, listened, caught a rustle from the hutch, and felt your cool fingers encircle it.

'Listen.'

Were you going to remind me how little care I had taken of you at the party that you hadn't wanted to attend in the first place? (And wouldn't have had it not been for your part in arranging the presence of the three poets.) But no, not only no word of reproach, but no reproachful silence either. You had other news for me, the best of all signs of forgiveness.

'I've just been talking to Liz; I couldn't leave her alone in the state she was in.'

'What state?'

'What state do you think? The state of having told you she was leaving and half-expecting some wonder that would save her self-respect and make it unnecessary, like Abraham not having to sacrifice Jacob at the last moment.'

'Abraham didn't try to have it both ways, that's the difference.'

'What a monster! To justify one of his frenzies of blood-lust (he seems to have had religious mania too) he claimed that God commanded him to slit his son's throat, but while he was sharpening his knife the fit wore off sufficiently for him to get his kick out of slaughtering a wretched goat that had got caught in some brambles.'

Your interpretations of the Old Testament were as imaginative, if less rewarding, as of the New. But I was anxious to return to the subject of Liz.

'In the end there was nothing for it but to make her a promise.'

'I see.' Though my mental reactions were sluggish at the time I couldn't think of an alternative to the fatal one that it was hard to believe you'd given her.

'What could I do?'

That was the sombre news that I was greeted with on waking and I could only take it in bit by bit. Liz was staying on with us: well and good, but what were you doing?

'I promised, among other things, I'd move into her room.'

'What other things, for sweet Jesus' sake?'

'She wanted to be sure there was no loop-hole left. I said I'd given my word, but if that wasn't enough for her I'd make it binding without any bible-holding act.'

'Herra, before we go any further into this, lock the door and come to bed.'

'I can't.'

'How can't you, if I call you by the names that touch you deepest: my hare's heart of wax, my little Mary M., my Rose of Picardy, and of Ismailia . . .?'

'I told her: "I promise by the desecrated body of Lazarella to have nothing more to do with him in that way."'

The blow had fallen, and you'd managed to make it

more terrifying by investing it with the solemnity of your vow. And still I could only advert to the consequences piecemeal or one by one, and not in the order of their importance: from now on I'd only see you clothed, at a minimum distance of several inches and never in the posture of abandon on bed or floor that had been my recurring vision of reassurance, the light of my darkness. The realisation of the greater loss, that of touch, came later and mostly in flashes of physical isolation and deprivation when I was outwardly fully occupied with our now functioning Hall of Freedom.

Everyone who came to use, or merely have a look at, the place expected something different.

One youth arrived with a manifesto he wanted put up that was headed: 'The Underground Group in Government Employment,' torn, he said, from a magazine called *Heatwave* and detailing all kinds of acts of sabotage.

'What repels me most,' he told me, 'about this place is the holiday atmosphere.'

Though it wasn't yet noon some young people were dancing in the former booking-hall to a pop record.

A middle-aged man in cap and steel-rimmed spectacles, a type I'd come to class as one of the older revolutionaries, took me aside and said: 'You're going to attract the armchair insurrectionaries, High-School dropouts, deserters from the movement and other self-styled heroes who'll turn the place into a doss house in no time.' He kicked a couple of broken bottles, left-overs from the previous day's celebrations, in confirmation of his prognostication.

'Hall of Peace and Companionship, is it?' asked somebody else, 'Hall of Idleness and Apathy, more like. Where's the dynamism coming from?'

Dynamism was the word I took in; it meant to me just

one thing: your caresses that had carried me up, up to unheard-of heights, on our Alpine ski-lift, to the dizzy point of momentary poise before the breath-taking downward swoop.

But Mullen had a big surprise: a clown not trying to be funny, the genuine, hilarious impersonator. You should have seen him expounding on the nine o'clock news and the advertisements that preceded it, but that week and the next you were never down in the Hall of Happenings that early.

He mimicked the manic ravings of the admen and then transported us to what sounded like the dream clinics with fully-carpeted, interior car parking where the executive manipulators spent the time between promotions having their nervous collapses, that they passed off as the flu, kept in some sort of check.

After news of a major speech by one of our elected representatives he gave a résumé of the gold-plated sincerities, the two-tone clichés and the hall-marked expressions of statesmanship with more conviction than the brothers themselves.

'That's what's so hilarious,' Mullen told me, 'he's the ideal citizen, the one in ten million, utterly got-at, conditioned and washed down the consumer drain into absolute, ecstatic acceptance of every public lie and prevarication.'

Maybe. But I didn't believe it. By pretending to be serious, and a mild type of nut case, his clowning preserved its genius.

You didn't come down that early because your presence was a signal for all the strays, mostly cats but a few dogs as well, to come out from the disused trucks and carriages (in one of which we had had our abortive tryst) where they slept, and this was best postponed beyond the hour when Mullen made his morning round. So you missed the discussions I had with him about the sort of place this should be.

That's what they all had a clearer idea about than I did, though they seldom agreed. As far as I knew, in spite of all the attempts, no alternative society was slowly spreading anywhere or looking like gradually taking over, as the early Christians had. Something must be lacking. *They'd* had the Crucifixion as still a fresh shock. But hadn't it been the news of the Resurrection and Christ's promise to return that had made them into such apparently confident, happy little bands? But wasn't that just another promotion job, a group-conditioning by the prospect of the sunshine holiday-in-the-sky to outdo all the later sunshine holiday advertisements? I'm telling you my private doubts, not coming to hard conclusions. Were they drugged and doped by the high-power campaigns of really great operators like St. Paul, publicists whose credibility was strengthened by their poverty, a sign of their sincere belief in the rosy future they were selling?

We've nothing like that, except the poverty, the poets and novelists, I mean. All we have are our insights into the Crucifixion, not much on which to found an alternative society!

Not much to offer as a substitute for all the bargains on show elsewhere!

And speaking of the Crucifixion, a woman who Mullen said had been the local librarian until the library had burnt down asked why there wasn't a crucifix anywhere.

'Because nobody would notice it; it has become just a piece of conventional furnishing like a mock-tudor chest in the hall. It's even more useless, you can't keep anything in it. It doesn't symbolise value for anything, unless, that is, an enterprising agency took it over as a shock-promotion gimmick with the caption: "This day you can be in the paradise of Majorca with me for as little as . . ."'

But in the middle of even the more absorbing of these discussions my own private and grievous loss would come back to me and I'd lose the thread of what I was saying and, instead of some satirical comment on the state of society, there'd pass through my head: 'Roses are blooming in Picardy, but there's never a rose like you.'

TWENTY-NINE

Next day . . .

'Next to what? You haven't mentioned a day or a date in the last half-hour.'

Next to a lot of minor events that took place when the station became Heartsease Hall.

One afternoon the phone rang (we had now an extension in our quarters, whether tapped or not, as you suggested, I don't know) and it was the sergeant to tell you he'd found homes for two of the leverets and if you brought them to an address a little beyond the barricade he'd be there to take them.

In the increasing number of confrontations between military and guerrillas the streets adjoining the no-go areas were particularly unsafe and the finding of homes for a couple of small animals wouldn't come sufficiently high on the list of security priorities to ensure the ones you would pass through being cordoned off.

But at least they were small enough to be carried in a shopping bag; you wouldn't have got far with anything that looked as if it might contain an explosive device.

'Be as quick as you can.'

Did your hair need all that brushing before you were fit to pass down two partially demolished streets, or was it for the sergeant? The last thought was one of those rather mean ones that I'm apt to formulate at critical moments without taking too seriously, a form of nerves. You were nervous too and, though you'd made up your mind, weren't in a great hurry to be off.

I accompanied you to the barricade where the guerrilla on guard waved you through after an astonished glance inside the bag. I stayed with him till I saw you disappear across the littered no-man's-land and through the narrow passage between the wall of a gutted house and a sand-bagged, military post.

'A courageous kid,' the youth remarked. 'I recognised her at the hooley from her photo in the papers when there was all the fuss about her disappearance. Did she really run away to join us up here?'

Back at the Hall of a Thousand Flowers I looked into the men's dormitory (women weren't allowed to sleep on the premises, a restriction I had contested). Several of the bunks were occupied by old men who were also provided with one meal a day in return for part of their pension. I'd become friendly with one of them and I sought him out now.

We understood each other on certain topics in ways we couldn't have with people much younger, and probably not even with you. It didn't surprise me when he took a packet of pornographic cards from under his pillow.

'It's not that I'm hooked on them, Mr. Sugrue; I keep them as souvenirs or rather reminders, and I'd sooner had the subject been illustrated by an artist who would have treated it more reverently, if you follow me.'

I followed him all right: they were faded reflections

of past wonders, treasured as tokens of what had once really been his, whoever, including himself at times, might doubt it.

'It's not so much the act you miss,' I suggested, 'as the sweet company of women, the living with one of them in the heaven of diffused sexuality.'

Our talk helped me as much as him and I left his bunk marvelling at the chance (the sort of destined chance you mean by the word) that, late in my life, had given me such fullness of companionship.

Back in my (no longer our) room, the first thing was to look at the alarm clock and reckon how much of the time I'd allotted for you to deliver the leverets and return still remained. (Don't think I didn't suspect that this calculated schedule would have to be extended and extended as it proved more and more inaccurate.)

Another bout of waiting, and for all my experience in the art of patience (second only to Job's and his was practised in relation to the loss of personal health and possessions and, as such, of a rather crude sort) I couldn't keep up any pretence at calmness. Not that, had anyone been present, I would have betrayed this by a sign; with me, as you know, anxiety, pain and joy are almost all root with only a few, tiny flowers.

The old methods of distracting myself didn't work. I tried to break the closed circle of consciousness by imagining events taking place simultaneously in distant places with the aid of the ancient Baedeker. I attempted to concentrate on possible problems other than mine connected with trains just now departing from Continental stations that I knew.

No use. What if I did evoke Frankfurt's teeming platforms, follow a couple into the big restaurant where the delicious open sandwiches of tender, underdone beef sprinkled with chopped gherkins are served at any hour of the twenty-four, but where they'd only time for a schnapps at the counter before the woman took the 16.05 for Berlin-Frederickstrasse to rejoin her husband on the other side of the Wall? Weren't you at this moment on the far side of an equally dangerous wall?

I tried reading passages in a book by John Lodwick about his adventures in the last war as a member of a commando group called Special Services. Through him I had known so well I'd previously been able to involve myself in these incidents and had thus passed away some anxious afternoons or desolate nights. But now my thoughts were wandering down a sloping street leading to the main part of the town.

Twice I went to the barricade after telling Liz to be sure to answer the phone and take a message if it rang.

I named the hour at which I would put an end to the waiting, be let through the barricade and walk past the wooden-framed slit between the sandbags. I'd have gone to find you sooner if Mullen hadn't warned me that descriptions of those in apparent authority had been given to the military by an agent they had had at the opening of the Hall of Fraternity and that mine, as that of one of the speakers, would be among them.

'By the fictitious priest?'

The slightest encouragement and I was half-inclined to re-invoke my drunken fantasy.

'God, no! I attend his Mass every morning.'

Mullen the daily communicant, Mullen the incorruptible extremist; two aspects of the man that shaped his public image. He both chilled and attracted me; there, for a couple of minutes I'd actually forgotten to listen for you in trying, and once more failing, to make up my mind about him! And as if my concentration on it had been what delayed your return, at that moment you opened the door.

You were beside me and drawing breath from the same room; you held out the shopping bag rounded at the bottom to the shape of the leverets.

'I couldn't get near the place; there was a bomb-scare and the street was closed.'

I took out the young hares and then, in a daze of relief, went to the kitchen for cabbage leaves and delayed there to wash them under the tap.

When I returned you were undressing. I had to get down on my knees to put the leaves into the hutch where the leverets were hiding and which stood on the floor at the foot of the bed. I supposed, as far as I'd come to myself sufficiently to question what you were doing, that you were changing into jeans (some of your things were still in the cupboard).

Turning to place a hand on the bed to help me to my feet, you were stretched, right under my eyes, on it, naked.

'Oh, you don't know how difficult it was to get back! Seeing me hanging around so long, they got suspicious and didn't want to let me go.'

But that wasn't why you were offering yourself up to me, reminding me of how, on our imaginary holiday, you had floated on the tepid green water just under my eyes and mouth. Or, if the impetus that had made you run all the way from the barricade had impelled you as far as this, it was also helping you in saying what you were starting to tell me.

'What made it so dreadful for you was that by taking

you away that morning the police confirmed the doubts about our relationship you'd had from the start.'

I raised my head a few inches but you pressed it back to your breast. 'Wait till I've finished. It was after that that you compared yourself to some elderly Belgian king who got hooked on under-age girls.'

'That was a joke.'

'Keep your mouth where it was. An old man's shame and folly, that's how they'd made you think of it, sometimes at least. Oh, I don't say it couldn't have been like that, that was the risk; the greater the prize the greater the risk, as you as a writer must know.

'After that dreadful morning you'd never have restarted with me, left to yourself. No, don't argue, your mouth is speaking to me in another way all the time. It was I who brought us back to each other, with the ice-cream kisses and the pellets in the bath and in all kinds of cunning little ways that you never noticed.'

'Did you lock the door?'

'I think so, I don't remember; she'll have to get to know . . . You kept catching sight of yourself in the light of public opinion, like catching a glimpse of oneself in a distorting mirror. And you were half-afraid to grasp the quite extraordinary thing that had happened. I wanted to show you how unique and miles away from anything common or vulgar it was by comparing myself to Mary Magdalen, but it made you laugh.'

My 'it didn't' was imprinted silently on your belly.

'There are a few lines in a book of verse the poets brought with them to show us, only they couldn't show you because you were drunk. They're by Robert Graves who, they said, was older than you, about a very young girl:

"So unendurably circumstanced a pair
Clasped heart to heart under a blossoming tree
With such untameable magic of despair . . ."

'That's all I can remember; it's our blossoming rose tree, isn't it?'

Was there a knock? Perhaps not, this was now the communal room and Liz was looking in to see if you were back and she could lay the table for supper.

I got to my feet, as an ex-general or diplomat might report in their autobiographies of the high-spot in their career when the distinguished personage entered the apartment to award them the high honour. As for you, you turned your naked back.

I registered the outraged tone rather than what Liz said. I was so convinced and exhilarated by what you'd just been saying that I went straight over to the aggressive.

'Oh, you're a good citizen, Liz, a model member of the social order, you don't have to tell us that; you never get yourself into a position where there are no moral precedents to turn to and you have to make a judgment of your own. The afternoon of the Crucifixion you'd have been tucked in bed with a hangover.'

THIRTY

We weren't long dressed and you were telling me I'd have to go and have it out with Liz (an uncomfortably vague way of putting it) when they came. I say 'they' not because I rank them with the enemy, but that's how I think of them: as namelesss messengers from the unknown with news they didn't suspect they were delivering and which I received (how could I not have?) no hint of.

The corporal was carrying a weapon I recognised as a sub-machine gun, though compared to those that I recalled it was like a car chassis minus the body-work, a portable object, in metal, of abstract art with grey and black undertones of a slaughterous theme. The sergeant, in loose jungle suit with bulging pockets, was saying to you as soon as he was inside the door: 'I was afraid you might have got hurt and rang the hospital but they hadn't anyone of your description; then I rang here half-an-hour ago to see if you were back but the fellow I got onto wasn't very co-operative.' (Since we had the extension, when the phone rang in the former station master's office, whoever answered it was supposed to switch through a call for us.)

The sergeant seemed to be saying that a bomb had exploded in or near the house whose address he'd given you.

'Come on, Corporal.' The sergeant raised his hand level with the badge on his beret and turned to the door. You caught his arm.

Had you an uncanny inkling that word had got to Mullen of the intrusion and that he'd send some of his men to the Hall?

'We'll come down with you.'

Why, when never so much had depended on them, were my wits less acute than yours? (Ah, the litany of meaningless whys that echo through the emptiness!) The first hint I had of an ambush was when I saw the main hall, normally busy this hour of the evening, deserted. I had stopped at the foot of the stairs to turn you back when the air around us split a second before the reverberations shot from wall to wall. And hadn't died down when the corporal's desolate instrument joined in with a shattering clamour, the antiphonal response to the first sharp burst of diabolic verse of this Vespers, of which one of the obscene words-made-steel had pierced your tender flesh.

We moved you with useless gentleness into the narrow passage-way and in its half-shelter the sergeant and I, while the corporal kept watch, pulled up your blue jersey marked with the insignificant sign, no more than a moth-hole, of the inward destruction. The tear in your belly was oozing wet but there was almost no flow of blood. If I hadn't seen what a high-velocity bullet did to a lump of gelatine I might have hoped the wound wasn't a fatal one.

I suppose by the altered direction of the firing that I hardly heard it was evident to the sergeant that his companions from the jeep had engaged the guerrillas at the other end of the hall and that now was the chance for the four of them to get out, but he would have stayed with me if I hadn't convinced him that I preferred to be left alone.

I sat on the first stair with your head on my knees and the colt automatic that I don't recall the sergeant giving me in one hand, while the gun battle that I heard from far away continued. It had ended, in so far as I ever had a reliable report, in the soldiers escaping with one wounded after the two guerrillas had retreated up the platform.

THIRTY-ONE

It rained, rained and rained, three days and nights on end; then a misty, damp day or two and the clouds rolling in again low from the west. Yes, I'm back at the cottage and whatever there is to tell about the last days at the Laggan I'll insert into the report from here.

What among the memories unshared with you from up there should be recorded? Perhaps that from your grave there's a view of the estuary.

I asked Liz would she come and keep house for me (that's how I put it) and she nodded; she didn't refer to the arrangement again while we were there nor on the drive south. When I saw the rain falling through the still air on our arrival I was helped to an acceptance of your absence by imagining your gradual withdrawal behind the sibilant, semi-transparent curtain. When I stood once more at the kitchen window through which I could just see the granite slabs gleaming wet and silvery out of a growth of weeds, I knew that the further distance would always belong to you.

At first I'd an idea of living in the loft and leaving the cottage to Liz, but that would have reminded me of the last phase of my marriage, for while I associated Liz first and foremost with you, I could still imagine that if Nancy had returned from the dead she would have become not unlike Liz and I might undo the harm I had done her. So I only slept up there and gave most of it over to the hares.

I parted from Mullen without rancour on either side after the funeral, which he attended. He knew that the Hall would never now become either of the somewhat different places that he, on the one hand, and we, on the other, had imagined it as. He didn't ask me to stay, though.

When the weather improved (not that I saw it as that) I started to clear the overgrown garden.

I recognised the familiar prevailing weeds that had been obscurely flourishing since I'd dug here last with a pang that hadn't the sharpness of those produced by everything more closely associated with you.

Without your mother's support we were poor; I was going to get rid of the telephone when Liz told me about an advertisement she'd put in the paper that had resulted in her getting some children from a couple of families of local gentry as pupils. She had managed this while I was preparing beds for the spring and without saying anything until all was satisfactorily arranged, hours, payment, everything.

This was a Liz I didn't know, hadn't bothered to get to know, though I'd prided myself on coming close to her on another level. She was keeping very quiet, very much to herself. I had a feeling that her indignation and my angry response that last night was still between us.

One night, instead of retiring to my box of a room with a skylight, I went to the cottage living-room after we'd had supper in the kitchen and Liz took the book she was reading and opened it but her eyes, lowered to the page, remained motionless.

'Can't you forget that silly incident in the light of what happened soon after?'

'Not my part in it, Sugrue. Please be patient with me, if that doesn't sound as if I thought I was in some way on your mind, which I don't presume for a moment.'

'Do you find life here very lonely?'

'Of course not; I've been more lonely for I don't know how many years.'

Strange, the things I hadn't really grasped about her!

'We'll be isolated without a car.'

She didn't say anything to that, but neither did she take up the book that she'd laid aside at my first question.

'I'll fix Nancy's old bike so you can ride it to Mass or to the bus when you want to go to town.'

'I'm not in a hurry to go anywhere.'

All the same I took the bike from where it had lain for years in a corner of the garage and went over it bit by bit. renewing brakes and tyres that I walked to the village and back for on a clear, frosty day when Liz was having one of her first sessions with her new pupils.

I once looked in during a lesson to ask her something, and there they were. We looked at each other, Liz and I, nothing was said, not even about what I'd come for, but the moment our eyes met I realised there were times when the lesson became unendurable to her because at the opposite side of the table it wasn't you.

Where was I? Fixing the bike with cold hands in the garage with the sound of the hares scuttling in the loft above. Liz came to tell me lunch was ready; I didn't reply because I was holding a screw between the lips; she watched me a moment and said: 'It was once a Rolls and now it's a rusty bike.'

What to make of it? A casual comment on a fairly

obvious contrast, much as if she had remarked that the weather to-day was a great change from yesterday's?

If so, why the minutely but pleasurably vibrating nerve inside me? A signal had come from Liz, even if she hadn't been fully aware of sending it.

Manual tasks, in the garden or garage, were some respite from the pain of thinking and recalling. Now for the first time since the return here a thought passed through my mind that, though imprecise, was exciting.

How could Liz's chance remark (even if it wasn't completely chance) put me in contact with the world of sensuality that the keeping of the tryst with you, that you'd set such store by, that night in the disused railway carriage had failed to do? I was ashamed.

Later, I began to grasp things that you, never subjected to the old dishonesties, had taken as a matter of course, such as the break in the line of communication (in spite of all legends to the contrary) between the senses and the heart.

But I'm too old completely and easily to break with old attitudes and not to have been puzzled and ashamed at the time by what I'm going to recount.

I recalled the incident of the girl hitcher, increasing my self-doubts. After all I'd learnt from you about loving-steadfastness and long, faithful vigils, was I still not very different from the easily distracted, rather dissolute character speeding back from his wife's funeral? I did not dare stay down in the cottage with Liz most evenings, but when I climbed to my room, instead of reading, my imagination became a monitor for sensual signals being exchanged all over the world. As in the dreams I used to have before your arrival, I was soon involved in the sort of situations (never crude, nothing like those depicted in the old fellow's cards) that disturbed and obsessed me.

Only when, through the partition, I heard the hares thump with their long hind legs on the floor boards in the course of their nightly ritual of careering and skipping round the loft was your presence strong enough to put the phantom girls from the Limpopo or the Eskimo belles to flight.

Much later, the deep night silence was broken by the recollection of the sound, distinguishable from all others, of high-velocity bullets tearing a private world apart.

Having been asked to give a talk on the novel that I mentioned at the beginning of this report, to a women's association called, I think, Friends of Freedom, I went to tell Liz I'd be away in the city for a night or two.

She was standing at the table in the kitchen. She wasn't expecting me at that hour of the early evening, added to which my expression may have been more than usually serious (I needn't tell you my face is not at any time the smiling, genial kind). As I began to speak I saw her hand that was holding a bowl tremble.

'What's wrong?

'You don't have to say it; you'd like me to leave, I'm in your way; I come between you and the past and you'd sooner be alone.'

It wasn't so much the words that made me realise how my avoidance of her had been affecting her; they might, I suppose, have been an attempt to get from me a clear declaration to the contrary. It was the uncertain way she placed the bowl back on the table (as if back in one of her hangovers) and the monotone of her voice as if reading out her sentence of banishment.

I took her in my arms; as at that moment I could have taken almost anything female and on two legs. As a boy I'd had to make do with a horsehair mattress folded in two.

I'm not saying that comforting Liz was just an excuse to get her into bed with me (not that an excuse was necessary). There's no way of separating these feelings, the old moral distinctions, as you taught me, don't work any more if they ever did with any honesty.

'Oh, Sugrue, do you really want me?'

What, for Christsake, was she talking about, standing there naked by now, a strong, big-breasted body which I was staring at as if I'd never set eyes on such a wonder before!

The bed or the floor, whichever was simplest, but when she was stretched beside me (in bed as it turned out) she insisted on talking.

'If I could have been there too, not always left out on the other side of the door, or banished down here to the cottage that time you and she pretended the ladder had slipped. If I could have been there too, anywhere, in a corner with my back turned, not as a voyeur, just not always out in the cold; if you could have made a hutch big enough and let me creep into it and stay in the room with you like the hares.'

I tried to stop this extravaganza with kisses which only had the effect of intoxicating her further.

'What we're doing now isn't shutting out anything or anyone.'

'All I'm bloody doing is listening!'

'Have patience, for another half-minute, till I tell you how I imagine your wife, always left out like me, never hugged and kissed like I am now, never having her heart expanded by you. Oh, don't I know how easily hurt and loneliness turn to moral judgment and feelings of superiority.'

'You sounded so morally outraged.'

Would you believe it, she only stopped talking when she felt I'd switched the line between us from word of mouth to touch of flesh! Then she laughed, as they say Lazarus laughed when he stepped out into sunlight.

'Don't skip the sexy highlights.' I can't help still imagining possible interruptions from you.

There weren't any, nothing unique, that is. Once the wave of sensation gathers towards its peak it's much the same where, how or with whom. Not that with Liz there weren't some variations in the preliminaries; I'm thinking of her laughter that suggested to me an eerie sea-sound, borne on the wind, as a marine creature, stranded between two tides, feels itself once more submerged. And then there was the phone ringing.

It couldn't be you, so let it ring. But Liz got up to answer it; she may have suffered a sea change but she hadn't lost her sense of responsibility. Perhaps, too, she liked the prospect of starting all over again.

'Oh, the Friends of Peace, is it? Good evening. The fact is he's got involved with another group, The Friends of Sex, and will have to postpone the talk to a later date.'

This was a Liz I'd never known nor dreamed of. I'd never really taken note of her before and this wasn't only due to you. I hadn't noticed her the time she'd been a student in my class. Not even to the extent of finding out her name and addressing her in my thoughts (as I had some of the others): Elizabeth, you're not an outstandingly bright girl, nor one of the prettiest, but you seem a serious person with some humour of a very personal kind.

To get back to what we'll call the matter in hand: Liz was wonderful. But at that point in love-making wonder descends from heaven and transforms them all. The grubbiest little tart or roadside hitcher turns into a seraph for five or six minutes.

The aquarium was on the bedside table; I came in and wound the watch every evening and carefully placed it again among the greenery as the tiny clock tower that told what was once our private time. We had hardly come to ourselves when Liz raised herself from under me and turned her head as if she wanted to see how late it was.

'That was the only place the child could look without being afraid of what she might see.'

Yes, she was off again.

'Outside of her water garden was one big Calvary where she'd been all alone till she met you. Many a morning at school I couldn't look at her face among all the others so well-adjusted looking and full of *joie-de-vivre*.'

She reached out an arm and took from the table drawer a newspaper cutting.

'When the saints of old fasted and wept over their crucified Lord their faith gave all the pain and torture a sense and purpose, but what did this poor child have to console her in her reflections?'

She handed me the cutting about coursing you'd kept with the others and, although I almost knew it by heart, I read it again.

'Eventually the dogs were caught and, in one case, the hare was loosed from the dog's mouth but not properly killed by the man who caught it, and a stick had to be used to kill it. In the other case the poor savaged body dropped to the ground and found the strength to hobble away from the torturers. . . .'

'It's hardly the moment. . . .'

'If we just lie here in each other's arms in oblivious

bliss till it's time to get up and go about our separate occupations we're as far away as ever.'

'What more do you want?'

'I'm talking too much; I won't next time, you'll see. It's the shock and the joy, Sugrue. What more do I want? Nothing, except never to forget.'

O LEPUS TIMIDE HIBERNICE!